The technique of editing 16 mm films

John Burder

Focal Press
London and Boston

Focal Press
is an imprint of Butterworth Scientific

First published by Focal Press Ltd, 1968
Second edition 1969
Third edition 1971
    Reprinted 1972, 1975
Fourth edition 1979
    Reprinted by Butterworths 1982
Fifth edition 1988

British Library Cataloguing in Publication Data

Burder, John
    The technique of editing 16mm films.–
    (The Library of communication techniques).
    1. 16 mm films. Editing – Manuals
    I. Title   II. Series
    778.5'35
    ISBN 0-240-50000-8

Library of Congress Cataloging in Publication Data

Burder, John.
    The technique of editing 16mm films / John Burder.–5th ed.
    135 p. 23.4 cm. – (The Library of communication techniques)
    Includes index.
    ISBN 0-240-50000-8
    1. Motion pictures–Editing. I. Title II. Series.
    TR899.B8   1988
    778.5'35–dc19

Laserset by Scribe Design, Gillingham, Kent
Printed and bound in Great Britain by
Hartnolls Ltd, Bodmin, Cornwall

Preface to the fifth edition

Editing is one of the most important and creative jobs in the whole film-making process. If you do the job well you can make even an unexciting subject win and hold an audience's interest. If you do the job badly you could waste the skills of those who have written, shot and recorded the film. So editing is important. It is no coincidence that many of the most successful Film Directors have started their careers in the cutting rooms.

A lot has been written about the artistic aspects of the job. In this book I have concentrated on practicalities. If you are planning to start work in a cutting room, you will find in the following pages all you need to get your career off to a good start. If you are going to edit a film you will find it easier and more interesting if you start by getting a thorough knowledge of the mechanics of the job. This book, preferably used in conjunction with the Media Manual *16 mm Film Cutting* (whose author shall remain anonymous!), is designed to help young professional film-makers and film students to learn the practical skills of film cutting.

In completely revising the text for this seventh reprint and fifth edition I have done all I can to ensure that it remains relevant to current cutting-room practice. Editors working with video should also find the revised text helpful. I am delighted to see the names of people who have been kind enough to tell me they found earlier editions of this book helpful now appearing regularly on television as editors and assistants. Throughout the book, the masculine gender rather than the more laborious 'persons' has been used for convenience and consistency, although the various jobs are carried out by women and men.

Making a film is, in my opinion, a very practical art. Although much can only be learned by practice, I hope this book will provide a sound basis for practical exploration.

John Burder

The library of communication techniques

Film

The technique of documentary film production
W. Hugh Baddeley

The technique of editing 16 mm films
John Burder

The technique of film editing
Karel Reisz and Gavin Millar

The technique of the professional make-up artist
Vincent J.R. Kehoe

The technique of the motion picture camera
H. Mario Raimondo Souto

The technique of special effects cinematography
Raymond Fielding

The technique of film production
Steve Bernstein

Television

The technique of lighting for television and motion pictures
Gerald Millerson

The technique of special effects in television
Bernard Wilkie

The technique of television news
Ivor Yorke

The technique of television production
Gerald Millerson

Sound

The technique of the sound studio
Alec Nisbett

The technique of radio production
Robert McLeish

BKSTS Dictionary of Image Technology

Contents

The pictures you will work with

Editing is one of the most important stages in making a film. A production which has been well shot and brilliantly directed will be a total waste if it is put together badly. On the other hand, one which has been shot well but without any particular distinction can sometimes be improved by skilful editing. As an editor your job is to give the film a definite pace. You must ensure that each shot is of the right duration, follows the preceding one smoothly and changes at the right point in the most appropriate manner. A good film editor combines artistry and technique so that a film flows from beginning to end without any abrupt interruptions or unevenness of any kind. You must retain the interest of the audience throughout the film.

You will also have to prepare a detailed soundtrack containing not only dialogue but music and sound effects, and you will be responsible for the progress of the film from the time the processed camera original is printed to the moment when the first copy of the final edited version is shown to an audience. It's a fascinating job and a cutting room is a first-class training ground for any would-be directors.

If you are going to produce a well edited film you must first be presented with suitable raw materials to work with. The film must be planned, scripted and photographed in such a way that it can be put together satisfactorily, or you will find you are faced with a hopeless task from the outset. Continuity errors must be avoided; the right pictures must be photographed from the right angles; suitable sounds which can be assembled into a composite soundtrack must be obtained. So let's give a few minutes' thought to those points which need to be considered before you start work: points which can have a great bearing on the outcome of your efforts.

Continuity and cutting

When a film is being shot, close attention must be paid to all aspects of continuity. In a large-scale production one person or more is made responsible for watching continuity points. Video recordings are often used to help with the work. In many lower-budget productions it is up to the director to ensure that continuity rules are correctly observed. An experienced, observant cameraman can help. If they are shooting a number of scenes designed to be edited together as a continuous sequence it is essential that they note the exact positions of all the actors and props at the beginning and end of each shot so you can match those points when you cut from shot to shot in your cutting copy. Obviously, it does not matter when the scene changes from a shot showing one subject to one showing something completely different, but if the same subject is observed in two shots which have to be edited together continuity is very important. If mistakes are made when the scenes are filmed you will soon discover them in the cutting room. Let's consider some examples of the sort of problems you may find.

Attention to detail

Suppose there is a script calling for shots of two people sitting in a café drinking coffee. They are talking to each other; the sequence consists of a shot showing both people at the same time, intercut with a close-up of one of them. When the action starts the person on the left is talking and the one on the right is listening. The one who listens holds a cup in his left hand. In his other hand he holds a spoon, which he uses to stir the contents of the cup. He looks at the man who is talking to him and then down to the cup.

In the second shot, the camera has been moved to concentrate on the man who is listening. We don't see the other character at all. The man listens, stirs his coffee and then answers the other fellow. The two shots were filmed separately, with a 20-minute gap in between. In that time an extra light was set up to fill in shadows which were not apparent from the first camera position. When the actors returned to the set for the second shot to be filmed, the man who was to be seen in close-up was worried. He could not remember if he was holding the cup in his hand or if it was still on the table. Had he started to stir the sugar? He could not remember. Fortunately for you the director could. He was aware of the importance of continuity, so when the long-shot was filmed he waited for the point at which he knew he was going to want to cut from one shot to the other and made a mental note of the position of the man's cup and hand. He could therefore make sure that the cup was held in precisely the same way and that the man himself was looking in the right direction at the cutting point. Small points, perhaps, but ones which are extremely important to you in the cutting room. When you cut those two shots together you will quickly spot any continuity errors, but by then it will be too late to do anything about them. If the listener is looking up in the long-shot and down in the close-up, or stirring his cup fast in one shot and slowly in the other, you will have a problem.

How a simple error can prove expensive

I remember one particular film unit which spent an entire morning filming an interview with a retired General. In the afternoon they decided to re-shoot some of the sequences they had filmed in the course of the morning. They took great care to set up the camera at a different angle, so that the shots exposed during the afternoon could be intercut with those taken that morning. Unfortunately no one noticed that during the lunch break the General had changed his tie. When the material was processed and screened the difference was blatantly apparent, and it was clear that the two batches of film could never be intercut. In that particular instance the film company was to some extent fortunate for, after some persuasion and another good lunch, the General agreed to be interviewed again and everything was re-shot, but of course it was a financial disaster because they had to meet considerable extra cost simply because no one had paid attention to one of the simplest points of continuity.

Change of camera angle

In the examples I have given above you will note that I pointed out that the film crew took care to change the angle of the camera's viewpoint from shot to shot. From your point of view that is important: your needs should be considered when a shooting script listing camera positions is first prepared. Audiences are easily bored: to maintain their interest the scenes they watch need to be changed frequently. If an entire scene is shot on a wide lens from one viewpoint audiences will soon find it hard to concentrate and will lose interest. For example, if a stage play were to be filmed with a camera set up in the middle of the auditorium showing the whole stage, you do not need much imagination to guess how boring the resulting film would be. So in writing a camera script every scene needs to be observed from a number of different positions and the audience's viewpoint must be changed frequently. That presents little problem when the script calls for different places or scenes to be seen one after the other. If, for example, scene one shows a long-shot of Kennedy Airport and scene two the World Trade Center, there is clearly no common factor in the two scenes and continuity does not matter. But when the same subject is to be seen for any length of time the angle of observation needs to be constantly changed. Even a simple sequence needs a variety of different shots if it is to look interesting on a screen—long-shots, close-ups and medium-shots taken from a variety of different angles. Now when a script is written those viewpoints must be carefully thought out with your needs in mind. If you cut from a view of one person to another view of the same person taken from almost exactly the same angle and distance it will look wrong. The action will jump and look unnatural; but that does not mean the whole action must be completed in one shot. It simply means that where a cut is to be made a change in the angle of observation is required. The script must specify what is needed and the scriptwriter must always bear in mind what you have got to do.

Continuity excuses

You can never cut two shots together satisfactorily if they show the same subject and are taken from an almost identical position. You must first go to an alternative view and then if necessary cut back to the original shot. In practical terms, for example, if you are cutting an interview and the film unit has just shot the person being interviewed and the director decides he does not like part of that person's answer and wants to lose it, you will be in trouble. If you simply cut out the offending sentence the cut will jump and the results will be unprofessional. If the director knows what he is doing he will have shot what is known a 'reverse' – a shot of the person conducting the interview. That person will have been filmed asking his questions and then simply standing or sitting where he was when the interview took place, nodding and listening without saying a word. You can then insert that shot at the point where the director wishes to lose some words. Start with the first shot showing the interviewee for the first part of his answer. Cut where the director wishes to lose words and insert the reverse – the shot of the interviewer. Run the edited track of the interview over it and at an appropriate point cut back to again show the person being interviewed. That intermediate reverse shot is being used as a 'cutaway'. Cutaways can get you out of a lot of trouble, as we shall see again later. If you are to be able to do your job properly it is essential they are filmed when shooting takes place.

Let's consider another example.

Matching the action

Another film unit has been out shooting scenes showing a man cleaning his car. They have taken two shots – a mid-shot showing the man and his car, and a close-up of the roof being polished. In the first shot we see the man and the car. He is facing from left to right. His hand is holding a cloth with which he is polishing the roof of the car. He is looking down at the cloth. Now if you are going to be able to cut those shots together smoothly the action at your cutting-point must be precisely the same. The cloth must be seen to be being used in the same way in the close-up as it is in the mid-shot. If it is moving in a different direction or at a different speed, when you cut from shot to shot it will look odd. So the action must be matched when the scenes are filmed so you can select the best cutting-point and join the two shots together without any jump in the action.

There is another continuity point which needs to be considered. If, after the mid-shot and the close-up in the example I have outlined above, the action were to return to a wider view, that shot would need to be photographed from an acceptable viewpoint. There are plenty to choose from. There are distant shots, long-shots, medium-shots, close-medium-shots, close-ups and big close-ups. The man cleaning that car was featured in the action of both the shots we have just considered, though in the second view we saw only his hand. He can be observed from the front or the side, from above or below, but the direction must be carefully thought out when the scenes are filmed. He can look towards the camera or away from it, from left to right or vice versa, but the camera must not be moved to the opposite side mid-sequence without an intermediate cutaway being filmed. If he is seen looking from left to right in one shot and right to left in another, filmed from a similar distance and intended to follow immediately, it will look very odd when you cut the two together.

Eyelines

When people appear in shots the eyelines of the subjects being filmed must always be considered. That is particularly important when you are intercutting mid-shots and close-ups, and also in interview situations. Take that interview we discussed a few minutes ago. You remember there were two shots to cut together, one showing the interviewee, the other the interviewer. The latter (cutaway) shot may have been filmed without any sound, with the interviewer just nodding. I have already explained how you can cut from one shot to the other without a jump by inserting the cutaway, but you will not be able to do that unless you have a suitable cutaway to work with. Continuity will again be a prime concern. The smallest lapse can make your job impossible. If, for example, the person being interviewed is looking from left to right when he is filmed, then when shots of the interviewer are taken he must be seen looking in the opposite direction, namely right to left, as if facing the person being interviewed. If the shots are taken from the wrong side, when you cut them together the interviewer and the interviewee will both appear to be looking in the same direction at some object the audience cannot see: the whole interview will look absurd. It happens regularly, as you will discover in the cutting room. So, next time you get a director who is inexperienced bringing rushes which cannot be satisfactorily cut together into your cutting room you may care to show him these paragraphs and invite him to spend a few days with you considering your problems. Then perhaps there will be no difficulties on future occasions. It is a good idea for trainee directors and cameramen to spend time in cutting rooms. They will find it helpful in their own jobs. It is no coincidence that many of the most successful directors started their careers as trainee assistant film editors.

Overlapping action

When filming is going on it often pays to overlap each shot forming part of a sequence of actions. The final action of the outgoing shot should be retaken at the start of the incoming one; dialogue immediately preceding the cut can be retaken too. It will make your life easier and give you more freedom in selecting your cutting points. That only applies in cases where several shots in a sequence feature the same subjects at the same locations. Let us consider some examples.

Three people are drinking in a bar. The script calls for three shots. The first is a general view of the bar in which the people are drinking. The second shows the group from a different viewpoint, and there is a third in which only the leader of the group is featured. As the action proceeds the men exchange empty glasses of beer for full ones. The long-shot is filmed first. When the second shot is taken from a different viewpoint the last actions taken by the men in the long-shot are repeated. There are two reasons for this: you will be able to choose precisely the right point to cut from scene one to scene two without it looking as if the actors are waiting for a cue; and the actors will also feel more at ease starting with an action they have already performed.

When shooting is completed

So, hopefully, you will find that the materials you are going to need to do your job properly have been considered from the outset. A script will have been produced listing shots which have been filmed from a variety of angles designed to be cut together at the appropriate points. Every day when shooting has been completed the film exposed in the camera will be sent by the camera assistant to a laboratory to be processed. The film will be accompanied by a copy of camera sheets made out by the assistant while filming has been going on. Those sheets will ask the laboratory to process the master film and print a rush print for editing purposes. They will also specify the length and number of every scene and take, and convey any special comments the laboratory or you may need to know about. Another copy of the camera sheet will be sent to you; we shall be considering how it can help you in a later chapter. The laboratory will develop the film exposed in the camera (the Master) and provide you with a rush print. 'Rushes' (the US term 'dailies' is also widely used) take their name from the fact that first prints are usually produced very quickly – often overnight, and thus in a rush.

Viewing rushes

Most directors like to view rushes every morning, so that if any scenes need to be re-filmed action can be taken before sets are dismantled or artistes dismissed. There can be many reasons for re-shoots. When a director sees the rushes he may decide that a performance which looked all right when the scene was filmed does not come across well enough on the screen. There may be microphone boom shadows on the background which no one noticed, or there may be technical faults on the film itself. Stock faults are rare but they do occur. Processing problems are not unknown, though fortunately they too do not occur very often. After 20 years spent directing films as well as editing them I have only once had to re-shoot because of a processing problem. It was a very expensive exercise. The scene was a big one for which we had taken over a disused hospital ward and hired in all the furniture needed to make it look as if it was in everyday use. There was a large cast too. In the action a patient lost her temper and raised hell with everyone. It was a very dramatic scene and one which went extremely well, but when we saw the rushes the following morning, there was a slight intermittent flicker. Subsequent investigation showed that a drainage outlet in a processing tank had become blocked, restricting the circulation of the developer. The fault had damaged the negative. Most people probably would not have noticed the fault, but as professional film-makers we did, and there was no doubt in our minds that the scenes must be re-shot. It was an expensive exercise, but when the film subsequently won several awards we were glad we had not compromised on quality. So, rushes can serve a number of different purposes!

A rush print will show errors like the one I have just described, but it should not be regarded as a guide to the quality of the results you can expect from a final show print. When show prints are produced the exposure and colour correction of each scene is carefully assessed before a copy is printed. When rush copies are made complete reels are often printed 'at one light', giving the same exposure and colour balance for every scene. Rushes simply give an indication of what each scene will show and provide you with a cutting copy (or work print) for editing.

Master materials

The term 'master' is a pretty wide one. I have used it above to describe the material actually exposed in the camera, but the description 'camera original' is just as appropriate. In the course of your work you will come across the word 'master' used in other contexts. You will find there are master soundtracks. They are the tracks which are the master recordings from which subsequent copies can be produced, and they should represent the ultimate in quality. The important thing to remember about any master film is that it is extremely difficult and often impossible to replace. It is thus very valuable. Student film-makers are sometimes tempted to shoot on a reversal film stock like Ektachrome and edit the master. Now working like that may sound all right when you are working on a tight budget. You will certainly save money by not printing a rush print and thus making a copy for editing purposes, but it is a false economy and one which should be avoided at all costs. When you start cutting you are bound to make mistakes. We all do, and as our careers progress we continue to do so. Only a Complete Disaster believes he never makes an error. So, you will probably want to change your mind about some of the points at which you want to cut. That's inevitable, and it's a good thing, for no editor, however experienced, makes every cut perfectly every time. Now, if you are cutting the master material you will be in trouble from the start because every change you decide to make will be there for ever for all to see. So will all the dirt and scratches which are bound to accumulate as a result of physical handling while cutting progresses.

If you follow the normal accepted professional practice of cutting a rush print made from the master you will not have any trouble. When everyone is happy with the results of your work the master will be matched to your edited cutting copy in the laboratory. That will be done by matching numbers found on the side of the master film and thus duplicated on your copy. When the two have been matched scene for scene and cut for cut the matched master, which has remained untouched since the rush print was made, can be graded (timed) and printed on new, unjoined stock to make an optimum quality copy. If, however, you have been cutting the master, when you use it to produce copies all the altered cuts, the scratches and blemishes will be there on every copy. So, though it may be tempting to cut costs and miss out that intermediate cutting copy stage, it is very unwise to do so. On a professional production the situation should never arise.

Processing

Let's briefly consider what happens in a laboratory when film is processed. In the course of your work you will find you have to deal with a laboratory on many occasions, so it is important that you should have an idea of what goes on. Bernard Happé's excellent book *Your Film and the Lab* (Focal Press) answers every question you could ever want to ask and goes into much more detail than I have space for here; when you have gained some preliminary experience in a cutting room I think you will find it is worth reading. You will also find that when you are working in the industry many laboratories will show you round their premises and be glad to explain what takes place in each department. The more you know about their work the better you are going to be able to liaise at the various stages of cutting where lab work is required, so a visit is in everyone's best interests.

Composition of film stocks

Film itself consists of a celluloid base coated with a photographic emulsion. The emulsion is made up of silver halides set in a gelatin carrier. When silver halides are exposed to light they change, but the human eye cannot see the change until the film is processed. When film is developed the silver halides which have been exposed to light become visible. The developer is then drained off and the film immersed in a fixing solution, which washes away the areas of silver which have not been exposed to light. It can then be washed and dried in warm-air cabinets. When that has been done it is ready to be printed.

At the end of the development stage, negative film shows a negative image. To get back to the tones of the original scene the negative must be printed on a roll of positive stock. When that is done, using a printing machine in the laboratory, a light is shone through the negative film, re-exposing it on a positive stock designed for that purpose. The positive is then itself developed and fixed. Again the developer converts the silver halides which have been exposed to light to black metallic silver, but this time the parts which are being converted are the opposite parts to those converted in processing the negative master. In the second stage of developing the print, areas not exposed to light in the printer are washed away. The print is then washed and dried and a positive image with a full range of tones should result. That's the basis of neg/pos processing and printing. We shall look at other film stocks in a moment but let's just give a little more thought to the ways in which film is handled in the laboratory.

Commercial processing methods

Labs have to cope with a vast footage of film every day. Cleanliness and temperature are their prime considerations. A tiny speck of dust can cause havoc in a lab, and if dirt lodges in a printing machine or on a roller it can scratch a negative and ruin it for ever. When film is processed it is laced round rollers which are immersed in a series of large tanks. The film moves through the tanks at a fixed speed: first through the developer, then a wash and then fixer, more washes and finally through a series of warm-air cabinets where it is dried. The temperature of the liquids in the tanks and the speed at which film passes through them depend on the type of film being processed. In a high-temperature bath film will move at speed. Today most lab processing is done at high temperature so film can be passed through quite quickly, enabling the lab to handle more films in a day and make a bigger profit. In the ECN2 process used for 16 mm colour negatives, for example, baths of developer are often maintained at a temperature of 41 degrees centigrade. Film passes through at a rate of between 100 and 150 feet a minute.

Printing methods – contact printing

When the master has been processed it can be printed to make the rush print which will become your cutting copy. There are several different types of motion-picture printer. In some, negative and positive are held in contact with each other. Others focus the negative image on a positive film held in a separate gate. The former are known as contact printers, the latter as optical printers. In most continuous contact printers negative and positive are held in contact with each other on a large driven sprocket. Inside the sprocket there is a light which can be regulated to any one of 21 different intensities by means of a shutter between the light source and the film. The negative runs nearest the printer light with the base facing it, and the unexposed positive runs outside, base outwards, so the two film emulsions are in contact. The two reels of film pass through the machine at speed. Modern continuous printers usually print at around 480 feet per minute. It is thus essential to ensure that film is undamaged, with no nicked perforations or joins which are improperly made.

From time to time you may also come across another type of contact printing machine – the step or intermittent printer. It uses an intermittent mechanism to advance the two pieces of film through a gate in contact with each other. The film is moved by a claw and advanced frame by frame in much the same way as happens in a film projector. There are those who feel that intermittent printers produce a steadier image and better definition than the continuous type, but they wear out an original more quickly and, as they take longer to produce an end result, running at speeds of around 50 feet per minute, they are not popular and are thus not widely used in modern laboratories.

Optical printing

In the third type of printer you will come across – the optical printer–the two pieces of film are not held in contact with each other. The image is projected through optics designed to show a focused picture. The size of the image can be varied by altering the distance between the two pieces of film; this type of printer is used when films are enlarged or reduced in size. As you will see later, 16 mm films can be blown up to 35 mm and 35 mm originals can be reduced to 16 mm. In an optical printer sections of a frame can also be blown up to fill the whole frame size, and special effects can be

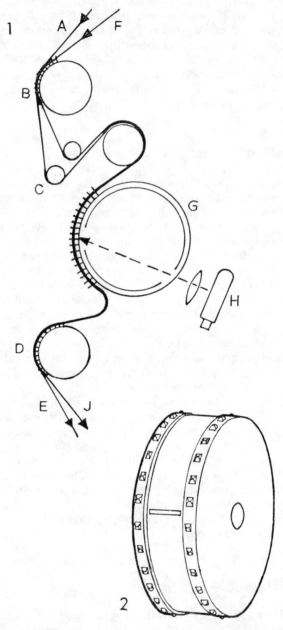

Printing cutting copies. 1, Continuous contact printer. Film from an unexposed reel of positive stock (A) meets the processed original (F) at feed sprocket (B). The two pieces of film then pass round tension rollers (C) to the main sprocket (G), where the new stock is exposed in contact with the original by the lamp and optical system (H). Finally, take-up sprocket (D) moves the film on to separate take-up reels for the original (J) and the newly exposed copy (E), which can now be developed.
2, Sprocket drum of continuous contact printer. The exposure aperture is formed in a fixed shell between rotating sprocket holes.

undertaken. As the image is projected masks can be interposed: such effects as views through keyholes and binoculars are often produced in this way.

So, the laboratory will process the master film and print your cutting copy using a continuous contact printer. If the production you are to edit has been shot on film it will have been photographed on one of the two different types of film stock which I have briefly mentioned in the preceding paragraphs – negative or reversal. How do they differ?

Negative and reversal characteristics

Exposed negative when processed shows a negative image in which the tones of the original are reversed, so if you film a black cat against a white wall on 16 mm black and white negative, the processed master film will show a white cat against a black background. To get the tones back to their original form the negative must be printed on a positive film stock. We have already seen how that is done.

An alternative way of working is to shoot on reversal camera stock. When a reversal master, like Ektachome, is processed the tones of the original scene remain the same throughout. They are not reversed at any stage, but that does not mean you cannot print a copy for editing. You can–by printing the reversal original on another roll of reversal stock using a printing machine in the way I have described above. A reversal original can also be printed on unexposed negative stock to make a duplicate from which copies can be made by using the neg/pos process, which is rather cheaper. We shall be considering both possibilities in detail in our final chapter. Some producers shooting on 16 mm like to work with reversal stocks. They claim the definition is better. If a 16 mm production is going to be blown up to 35 mm there are those who feel that it is best to shoot on a 16 mm reversal original, but as there is an excellent range of negative and internegative stocks available the argument is perhaps chiefly one of personal taste.

Black and white copies of colour originals

Today you will find that most productions originating on 16 mm tend to be shot on negative, so you are most likely to be working with a 16 mm colour cutting copy printed from a 16 mm colour negative; but don't be surprised if you are not. If the film you are cutting is being produced on a shoestring budget you may find your cutting copy is in black and white. Black and white rush prints are slightly cheaper than colour ones and if money is tight it is possible to economize by asking the laboratory to print a colour original on black and white panchromatic stock. Pan stock should always be used because it is sensitive to all the colours of the spectrum. In practical terms that means it will look reasonable, and if there is any edge fogging it will show up.

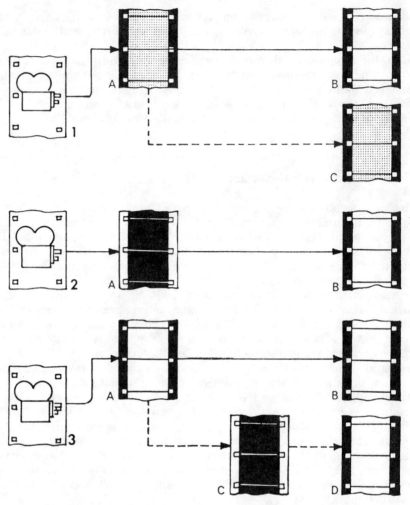

Production of cutting copy from originals. 1, From colour master: reversal processed (A); duplicated on black and white reversal stock (B); or duplicated on colour reversal stock (C). 2, From black and white negative (A), contact printed on black and white positive (B). 3, From black and white reversal: reversal processed (A); duplicated on black and white reversal (B); or printed on negative stock (C) which, when processed, can be printed on positive (D). If you shoot on colour negative the processed original can be printed on colour positive or black and white positive stock.

A choice of gauges

In the course of cutting you may also find you have to deal with material shot on other gauges or on video, so let's spend a few moments looking at the other formats you may encounter. Today professional productions are usually shot on 35 mm or 16 mm film or on videotape. 35 mm film is used for most cinema feature films and for many television commercials. It is the largest film gauge and the nicest to work with. As it is also the most expensive it is only used on productions where a good budget is available. Before the last war 35 mm was the only gauge used by professional film makers. 16 mm was described as 'sub-standard' and dismissed as 'spaghetti'. Today television thrives on spaghetti and, though video is taking over some jobs, television networks are still investing heavily in 16 mm equipment because it offers the best quality and the most versatile production techniques. In the hands of an experienced production team it can also be quite economical.

Working with different formats

Shooting on video has advantages and drawbacks and so does film. You will find there are people in the industry who will passionately defend their right to use one particular medium, dismissing the other as quite impracticable. In fact, as both film and video have their good points and their bad ones, there is a lot to be said for bringing the two methods together to produce an optimum quality product at the right price, and that is what many experienced producers are now doing. Why do they work that way?

Film or video – cost considerations

Film stock and processing are both quite expensive, but in the hands of an efficient crew, with a director who knows what he wants and what he is doing, and with a subject which is not open-ended, filming costs can be kept in check. There are some situations where a high filming ratio is inevitable, and on those occasions shooting on tape may be cheaper. Film enthusiasts would probably argue that any economies made in shooting are going to be lost in paying for increased video editing time, and in some situations they are right, particularly if the video edit is done entirely 'on line', using the most expensive equipment throughout. Video editing time tends to be costly largely because electronic equipment is expensive to buy and, as video technology is constantly changing, equipment manufacturers are always bringing out new models. Video hardware gets out of date very quickly. Companies providing a video editing service or hiring video cutting rooms thus have to spend considerable sums keeping abreast of the latest innovations. They also have to meet all the usual costs involved in running a business. Add to that the cost of paying the editors and engineers needed to run the operation and you can see why the cost of video editing time adds up. Film editing is often cheaper. The hardware needs to be replaced less often. There are no revolutionary developments or dramatic changes in technology. The machines you will find in cutting rooms today simply represent the latest refinements in equipment which in most instances has been in use for a good many years. Film editing is well-established. Video editing is still developing and that affects the cost producers have to pay at the end of the day.

Working with film and video

To get the best possible deal productions are now often completed using more than one format. Some programmes are shot on film and edited on tape. Others are shot on film, rough-cut on film and then fine-cut and titled on tape. Occasionally the reverse applies: programmes are shot on tape and edited on film. Film soundtracks are sometimes used in conjunction with a video picture and many films are sold on videotape so, if you are asked to edit a 16 mm film, you may well find at some stage you are involved in working with more than one gauge. So let's see how you can go about it.

Film formats

Let's start by considering the various film formats. 1000 foot of 35 mm film runs for 11 minutes and 7 seconds when it is projected at 24 frames per second and ten minutes and 40 seconds when it is shown at 25 fps You may perhaps think the seconds do not matter, but if you work in television you will soon discover their importance. TV networks calculate the running time of their programmes to within a few seconds simply because commercial breaks for advertising and regional 'opt outs' to local programming have to be synchronized very precisely. As I am sure you appreciate, when a TV programme is networked, not every part of the network shows the same commercials when an interval occurs. Individual stations opt out and insert their own commercials and then return to the main programme being transmitted by the network, so timing is crucial. A 30-second error can mean losing one commercial and all the advertising revenue arising from it. So to ensure frame accuracy film is measured in feet. You will find a detailed breakdown of footages and running times of 16 mm film at the end of this book. There are 16 frames in every foot of 35 mm film. There are 40 frames in a foot of 16 mm film and a 400-ft roll runs for the same time as 1000 foot of 35 mm film, so you can seen why 35 mm stock costs more to buy and to process.

You may also come across another gauge from time to time: 8 mm film was widely used by amateur film makers until home video came on the market. There are still a fair number of enthusiasts and for amateur film-making 8 mm can still be fun, but it is rarely used professionally.

No one really enjoys working with 8 mm. The pictures are difficult to see without projecting them on a screen and the film is fragile to handle. Sound is also a problem for there is no internationally standard procedure. Some 8 mm cameras shoot at 24 frames per second, which is the standard speed for shooting sound films on the other gauges, but others will only operate at 18 fps. (Productions destined for television are often shot at 25 fps.) For those reasons, and due to the revolution in amateur film-making brought about by the introduction of videotape, you are unlikely to come across 8 mm film very often in your career as a film editor. If you encounter it at all it will probably be in a situation where you are editing a film shot on 16 mm or 35 mm and the producer wishes to incorporate some film which was shot by an amateur.

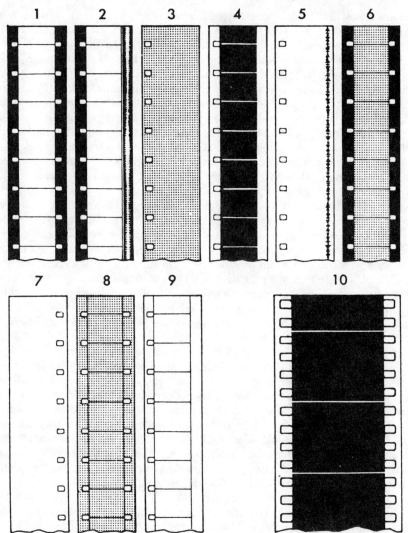

Types of film stock. 1, 16 mm mute positive. 2, 16 mm combined positive. 3, 16 mm magnetic. 4, 16 mm mute negative. 5, 16 mm optical sound negative. 6, 16 mm colour master. 7, 16 mm white spacing. 8, 16 mm colour negative. 9, 16 mm colour positive. 10, 35 mm mute.

Intercutting 16 mm and 8 mm

Imagine you are cutting a programme which has been shot on 16 mm colour negative. It's a television programme about airline security. The film crew have travelled around the world shooting interviews and action scenes on 16 mm colour negative. The film they shot has been processed and a colour cutting copy has been made for you. The uncut original negative is still at the laboratory and you are working with your 16 mm cutting print. You are getting along fine until one day the producer comes along and tells you he has been offered a remarkable bit of film shot by someone who was on a plane when it was hijacked. He was an amateur moviemaker who happened to have his camera with him when the incident occurred. During the hi-jacking he kept filming and now he has offered his amateur film to your producer, who is very keen to use it. There is just one snag. It is an 8 mm reversal film and you are cutting a production shot on 16 mm negative. The producer wants to use those scenes and is not really interested in your problems. What are you going to do about it?

Look at what you are being presented with and what you are going to need at the end of the day. You are being given an 8 mm reversal film and you have got to cut it into a 16 mm colour negative. All you have to do is ask the film laboratory to clean the 8 mm original and make a 16 mm colour blow-up internegative suitable for intercutting with original 16 mm colour neg. You will also need to ask them to make a 16 mm cutting copy from the dupe. They will load the 8 mm original on one side of an optical printer and a roll of 16 mm internegative on the other and expose one on the other. The 16 mm internegative will then be processed and a rush print made for you. Don't expect much in terms of quality. Blowing up 8 mm to 16 mm is very much a last resort, but when unique material can be obtained only in that way it can be done, and that is one way to go about it. There is an alternative.

If your programme is going to be finalized on videotape for television transmission there is another way which can give even better results. You can complete the editing of your 16 mm film and insert blank spacing at the point where the 8 mm material should occur. When your 16 mm cutting copy has been approved the colour negative can be matched to it and the laboratory can be asked to produce a graded (timed) showprint on low-contrast telecine stock. The print, together with your final mix master soundtrack, can be recorded on videotape. The 8 mm film can also be recorded on video and inserted, retaining your soundtrack at the point where the spacing occurs. If any fine adjustment is needed it can be done on tape. Working this way the quality of the 8 mm insert will probably be slightly better, but one way or the other you will be able to arrange to do what your producer wants, and that is what it is all about at the end of the day.

Intercutting 16 mm and 35 mm

So film formats are interchangeable. Let's consider another situation you may find yourself in. Perhaps you are working on a corporate film for a commercial sponsor. It has been shot on 16 mm colour neg. The original neg has been processed and printed and you are cutting a 16 mm colour rush print when the film's sponsor suddenly remembers that years ago, when the company headquarters was built, a newsreel company shot some film of the VIP opening ceremony. They would very much like to incorporate those scenes in the film you are now editing. Research shows that the shots they want still exist and can be made available. There is just one snag. They were shot on 35 mm black and white negative, so how on earth are you going to incorporate them in the production you are working on now? Again you will need to enlist the help of your laboratory. Ask the newsreel company to supply you with a 35 mm fine-grain dupe positive of the material they hold and then get your laboratory to make a 16 mm reduction internegative on colour stock suitable for intercutting with your 16 mm colour original. Be sure to tell them that you want to intercut it with original 16 mm material so that the geometry of the duplicate they produce will be correct. It is also important to tell them you are working in colour so they do not produce a reduction dupe negative on black and white neg stock. Colour stock is multi-layer and thus thicker; black and white neg and colour neg cannot be satisfactorily intercut.

When you have finished editing your production the producer may decide he wants to sell copies on videocassette or to produce 35 mm copies for showing in cinemas. Again these are situations which will not present you with any insurmountable problems. In the last chapter in this book you will find a detailed description of how to go about it and diagrams illustrating all the various interchange possibilities. But for the moment let's go back to the beginning of the editing process.

2

The sounds you will work with

We have so far considered the picture materials you will need to work with. You will also be concerned with sound. When audiences think of a soundtrack they probably think of a wavy line on the side of the film, but in practice there is a lot more to a soundtrack than they could ever envisage. Preparing a good soundtrack is part of your job, so let's see what you will need to work with and what the main stages of the job will be.

Working in a cutting room you will come across two different types of soundtrack – magnetic and optical. What are the advantages and disadvantages of the two types and when should each be used?

Optical tracks

For release prints – the name given to prints used for general showing rather than in the course of film production – an optical soundtrack is almost standard. An optical track is one which is printed photographically on the side of the film alongside the picture. On 16 mm film the actual frame area of one frame of film is 7.4 mm high and 10.41 mm across (in the camera gate); the soundtrack of an optical track on 16 mm film has a full width of 0.085 inch or 2.15 mm. Projectors only read part of this area: the actual sound signal is contained in an area about 1.8 mm wide, with masking on either side. An optical soundtrack is printed alongside the picture by a laboratory. It can be printed from an optical sound negative or duplicated from a reversal sound master track. Before the lab can do its part of the work you must synchronize the sound negative to the master picture material so the two can be printed together on the new print stock. (The sound on a 16 mm combined optical sound print–*comopt*–is 26 frames ahead of the picture.) We shall see how this is done in a later chapter. Practically all 16 mm sound projectors can show a film with an optical track. The majority of 35 mm cinema films also have optical soundtracks but magnetically striped tracks are used for special releases and for major presentations in key theatres.

Magnetic tracks

In the course of your work you will be much more concerned with another type of sound – the magnetic soundtrack. There are two types of magnetic sound – separate magnetic tracks (*sepmag*) and combined magnetic stripe (*commag*), which is also known as sound stripe. Let's consider that first.

Mag stripe, as the name suggests, is a magnetic soundtrack located on the edge of the film. On 16 mm film a magnetic stripe can be placed in the same area as an optical soundtrack as an alernative to it, or alongside so that both optical and mag stripe are available. Mag striped films are easy to recognize. The stripe itself is simply a stripe of brown ferrous oxide applied to the film. The main differences between a mag stripe track and an optical one are the quality of the recording and the way in which the sound is recorded and reprodued.

Optical soundtracks are printed, like picture negatives, by a photographic process. Magnetic sound has to be re-recorded magnetically from a master track on to either a fully coated magnetic copy or a mag stripe. You play the master mag recording on one machine and re-record on another. Again, sound synchronization must be preserved, as we shall see later. The sound on a 16 mm mag stripe print is 28 frames ahead of the picture. The audio quality of a mag recording is better than an optical one. There is less background noise and the range of sound obtainable is much greater. For that reason separate magnetic sound tracks are used throughout production; optical tracks are only encountered in the last stages of making copies for projection. Sound stripe copies are now comparatively rare.

Magnetically striped prints give better quality sound than optical ones, but, alas, there are very few projectors equipped to show them, so today mag striped copies are rarely used. Optical tracks are much more common. They are reproduced by shining a light through the optical soundtrack on to a photo-electric cell and thus to an amplifier. Mag stripe prints are reproduced by a magnetic replay head, but heads are not generally fitted to

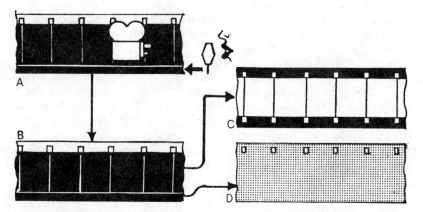

To make a striped sound print you can either shoot on sound stock and edit the processed master (A), or shoot mute (C) and print the picture mute and have it magnetically striped (B) whilst editing with a separate magnetic track (D), which can then be transferred to the striped picture.

standard 16 mm projectors. For that reason, until quite recently 16 mm films were usually seen and heard with optical soundtracks. Today many 16 mm productions end up being shown on video. When production is completed the master final mix magnetic sound and a low-contrast print made from the master picture material are re-recorded on video; the quality of the end result can be very good.

Separate magnetic soundtracks

In the course of editing you will use magnetic sound for all the main stages of the work but the tracks you use will not be on the side of the film. They will be separate ones (sepmag). Separate magnetic tracks are an essential part of practical editing. If you are working with a 16 mm picture you will probably use 16 mm magnetic soundtracks. Like the picture stock, mag sound stock has perforations, though they are on one side of the film only and not both, as is the case with some camera and print stocks. Magnetic sound is opaque. It's coated with ferrous oxide. You cannot see the sound as you can on an optical track. You have to play a mag track on suitable equipment to find out if there is any sound on it. For editing it has many advantages. By far the most important of these is its high original quality and relatively small loss of quality when it is re-recorded. In the course of making a film soundtracks have to be re-recorded several times. The master location sound is first re-recorded on perforated magnetic film for editing. When you have prepared your soundtracks you will go into a dubbing theatre and mix them together. When that is done the sound mixer may decide to premix all the music and sound effects tracks before re-recording them again with the dialogue or commentary. Each re-recording will be another stage away from the original sound. When the film is finalized the sound will be re-recorded again either on video or as an optical or magnetically striped soundtrack. So maintaining a high standard of quality at every stage is very important. Using separate magnetic tracks, quality can be safeguarded throughout.

Magnetic tracks are easily cut and joined and, if you make it carefully, the join is usually inaudible. When you join an optical track you will always hear a slight loss of quality when the splice passes through the projector. So when you are editing a 16 mm film you will find that the use of 16 mm magnetic tracks recorded on separate rolls of perforated magnetic film is standard practice. You will build up a whole series of soundtracks and edit them to match the action (the *cutting copy*). The tracks will consist of dialogue, music and sound effects. When they are all completed you will take them into a dubbing theatre and mix them together to make a final Master mix recording. That master track can be used to produce video copies, re-recorded on mag stripe or as an optical sound negative for printing comopt copies.

Sync or wild?

There are a number of other technical terms which you will need to know about when you are editing sound. You will need to know the difference between soundtracks which are *sync* and those which are *wild*. Sound is synchronized (editors say 'in sync') when it precisely matches the picture. Take an obvious example. Someone hits a nail with a hammer. If the sound of the action coincides with the picture you see, it is correctly synchronized and thus in sync. If the sound occurs before or after the person hits the nail, and thus makes the scene look absurd, it is out of sync. You have probably seen films transmitted out of sync on television. It does not happen very often but it does sometimes occur; when it happens there are usually some very red faces in the cutting room or telecine suite. Having a TV programme transmitted out of sync is an editor's nightmare.

Recognizing sync problems

If sound and picture are not correctly synchronized, a difference of even one frame will be noticeable. It will not feel right. We have all seen films where the lip movements of people speaking on the screen do not match the words coming from the soundtrack. 'Out of sync' is a term you will grow to dread. If you do your job properly and prepare a detailed soundtrack there will be many points at which synchronization can be checked. Such places are known as *sync points*. Every audible footstep, a door opening or closing, the striking of a match and many more sounds are sync points because the sound and picture must precisely match and be frame-accurate at that point.

Shooting sync sound scenes

When sync sound scenes are shot, sound can be recorded either on a magnetic stripe on the edge of the master film in the camera (*single-system sound*) or on a separate recorder locked to the camera by a synchronizing pulse (*double-system sound*). In studio shooting and on major productions that recorder may be loaded with 16 mm magnetic film. For most 16 mm productions, when double-system recording is used, sound is recorded on quarter-inch tape locked to the camera by a synchronizing pulse. Today the double system of working is almost standard, but I shall explain how the other system operates because you may occasionally still come across it.

Single-system shooting

When sync sound is shot using the single system, sound and picture originate on the same piece of film. The unexposed stock has a magnetic sound stripe on it and the location sound recordist channels his recording directly on to that stripe inside the film camera. When shooting has been completed the film is sent for processing. The mag stripe, which is an integral part of the film, is thus processed with it but the processing does not affect the sound recording. If the film has been shot on striped reversal stock, when it has been processed it can be shown straight away as a commag print. For years that is how rush television news stories were shot and how many sporting events were recorded. It is not an ideal way of

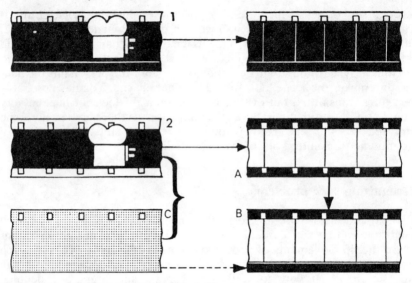

Ways of editing a striped sound recording. 1, Shoot on magnetically striped stock, making a simultaneous striped recording. You can edit the processed master. 2, Shoot on striped stock and transfer striped sound from processed master to separate magnetic and edit both, using picture as mute.

working. You are handling the master throughout and, as sound is recorded on a mag stripe 28 frames ahead of the picture, it is difficult to edit, but for years that method of shooting enabled TV companies to show things they would not have been able to get on a screen in time if they had used the slower double-system method of shooting, where sound has to be re-recorded before it can be edited. You may occasionally come across single-system shooting today, particularly if you find yourself working in Third World countries, but in most places video has taken over the jobs which used to be done in this way. If you do find you have to work with a single-system original you can either cut it as commag print, remembering that 28-frame sound advance, or have the stripe re-recorded on separate magnetic film and then cut it in level synchronization, which will give you much more cutting freedom.

Double-system sound

You are much more likely to find you are working with sound which has been shot double-system and originated on quarter-inch tape. Before you can start work the master tape must be re-recorded (*transferred*) to 16 mm perforated magnetic film by a sound transfer studio. While that is being done the master picture material can be processed. Orders for carrying out that work will probably be issued by the camera assistant for the picture master to be processed, and by the sound recordist for the master tape to be transferred. You will simply receive the resulting reels of film and copies of the camera and sound sheets. You should look at those sheets before you do anything else because they could save you a great deal of work. If you do not look at the sheets you could waste hours trying to find material which does not exist.

Printing selected takes

When a master film is processed, the whole of the original has to pass through the processing baths, but when a cutting copy is printed it is perfectly possible to omit scenes and print only selected takes. If there are a lot of long scenes and the director knows some of the takes are going to be useless because the actors' performances were poor or because there was a technical fault, he may well ask the cameraman to tell the lab to print only selected takes. The cameraman will circle those takes on his camera report sheet and instruct the lab to process all the master but only print the selected takes he has specified. The sound recordist can likewise ask for only selected sound takes to be transferred. So, look at the camera and sound sheets and see what has been ordered before you start work: then you will not be surprised when you look at the sound and picture rushes.

Non-sync sound

Not all sounds are synchronized or intended to be so. Background noises do not have to be frame-accurately synchronized and dialogue spoken out of the view of the camera does not have to be lip-synchronized either. Commentaries (voice-over narration) are frequently recorded 'wild' – the name given to sound recorded on equipment working independently of the camera. If the film you are editing does not involve synchronized speech it may well have been shot without a sound camera. Indeed it may have been shot without any sound at all, and the job of creating an entire soundtrack will thus have been left for you in the cutting room. You can cut the picture first without any sound at all and when the action has been finalized you can add a commentary, music and sound effects. Creating a soundtrack from nothing can be great fun and it is well worth doing the job properly. Too many films are thrown together with a little hackneyed music added when there isn't any commentary, or wall-to-wall words which make audiences mentally switch off a few minutes after the film starts. It is easy to forget that films consist of two main elements – pictures and sound: if a soundtrack is used creatively it can do much to enhance the quality of a film. A good film editor will take immense care to find the right sound effects and use them in an interesting way to win the attention of an audience and retain it throughout. Later on we shall see, stage by stage, how a soundtrack can be prepared.

Materials you will need

A decision on the type of soundtrack the film will have must be taken in the early stages of pre-production planning. Again the budget will have a bearing on how that decision is made. In an ideal world, even if the production is a simple documentary, a camera capable of shooting sync sound scenes would be used for every shot and a sound recordist would be present at each location. He could then record any scenes which needed to be shot in sync and record background wild tracks at each location. The wild tracks will not precisely match the film shot by the camera, as the recording equipment and camera will not be synchronized when they are recorded, but you will be able to make them fit the picture in the cutting room. If wild tracks from each location are available it will make the finished film sound better and your job will be much easier.

If you are unlucky and the budget has not been able to meet the cost of having a sound recordist and appropriate equipment at every location you will have to obtain all the sounds you need elsewhere. You can probably obtain most of them from a sound effects library or from a dubbing theatre. It can be quite difficult to find good-quality recordings of anything but the most basic sounds, but if you know what you want and are determined to persist until you have a really detailed, good-quality soundtrack you will get there in the end. I once spent hours trying to find a recording which would sound right for a shot of a mechanical hoist lifting a car body on a factory assembly line. The film, about the designer of the Mini car, had been shot with very little sync sound. An interview with the designer had been shot in sync but the sound recordist had only been called in at the last minute when the television company discovered that they were going to be able to shoot an interview. When the interview had been shot he had to go on to another pre-arranged job while the camera crew went down to the production lines and shot scenes of the cars being made and of the designer walking round inside and outside the factory. Those scenes were all shot without sound but when projected they looked unreal without it. As the editor responsible for the programme I was determined to bring the scenes to life and find the right sound effects. I managed to get good interior and exterior car factory background sounds from several different sources and then turned my attention to the detail in the shots. I managed to find sounds for most of the machines which were prominently featured until I came across that mechanical hoist. Eventually I found a recording of a household food mixer, played it at the wrong speed and cut it to match the movements of the hoist in the picture. It worked superbly and sounded just right.

Using wild tracks

You will find that wild tracks recorded on location and sound effects obtained from other sources can bring a scene to life, but how do you use them when you are editing a film? Where there are dialogue scenes you can use them to even out the background and where there is no dialogue they can speak for themselves, drawing attention to items of interest. Let us consider these two applications in a little more detail.

Imagine you are editing a dialogue sequence filmed in a busy street. An interviewer is questioning passers-by on some topic of interest. When you cut you will probably have to assemble a number of different shots of the interviewer and various people being interviewed filmed as sync sound takes at various times in the course of a day. The cameraman will have photographed the action on mute film stock (the master), which will have been processed and printed to make your cutting copy. Sound will have been recorded on a separate recorder using quarter-inch tape, and that master tape will subsequently have been re-recorded on perforated magnetic film. Now you may well think that because you have got synchronized sound for each shot you do not need any wild tracks, but you will soon discover that that is not the case. When you cut the picture of those interviews together you will also cut the sound, but remember that those scenes you are cutting were filmed in a busy street. There may be quite a lot of noise in the background but the traffic is unlikely to have been consistent throughout the day. When some of the interviews were filmed it may have been heavy and when others were shot it may have been light. The level of the background will not be the same throughout. So, when you have cut the interviews together you will find the sound level varies considerably from cut to cut. The dialogue will make sense but there may be nasty bumps in the background. You can make the whole sequence sound much nicer by adding a wild track of constant traffic noise as an additional background sound. When you have finished editing you can go into a dubbing theatre, mix the tracks together and smooth out that difference in the background sound.

Bringing scenes to life

When a film is shot without any synchronized sound at all, wild tracks and library sounds may be all you have to work with. Let's again take a street scene as an example and consider what you can do. Imagine you are cutting a sequence which shows general activity in a city street. There is no sound at this stage, so take a good look at the picture. What exactly does it show? There are a number of cars and commercial vehicles moving along the street fairly slowly. A car appears to have broken down on the other side of the street and several other vehicles are held up behind it. There is also a bus stop: a bus draws up and stops for long enough for passengers to get on and off. It then moves off again; that is where you have cut to a shot filmed at another location. Without any sound at the moment that scene looks pretty lifeless. How can you bring it to life and what are you going to need to work with? You could leave it without any sound effects at all and just put a commentary over it. If you do that it will be slightly more interesting but still not convincing. It will be much more credible if you recreate the sounds of the original scene, and if you do that you will find you can have quite a lot of fun. You will need suitable wild tracks. Your first will be general traffic roar for the background. You will also need the sound of that bus stopping and starting. If you want to make a really good job of it you will then add some detail. On the far side of the street, where that motorist has broken down, cars are being held up. A few impatient motor horns might not come amiss, but they should not be overdone or they will become annoying. If there are people talking on the pavement a little chatter could be in order too. All these are small points but they add detail and in a soundtrack detail can mean life.

Some of the sounds you are going to need for that scene can be obtained from sound libraries or dubbing theatres. Traffic background and car noises are easily obtained but it is always better if they can be recorded by a location sound recordist. Wild tracks should be recorded whenever the budget permits. Background sounds can be very helpful when you are editing a soundtrack. We have already seen how in the case of those interviews filmed in a busy street a wild track enabled cuts to be made more smoothly. Let's consider another example.

Controlling background noise

This time you have got a sequence showing two people talking in a big factory. The scene has been shot with sync sound but the recordist taping the sync dialogue found the factory was so noisy that the background sound was making the words difficult to hear. To overcome this problem he gave the actors taking part personal microphones designed only to hear sounds made nearby. On the sync soundtrack you can thus hear the voices very clearly. The factory noise has almost disappeared. That is all very well but the scene does not look right with the clinically clean dialogue being spoken in such a busy place. There is a lot of activity in the background and the factory is clearly a very busy place. Here too a wild track can provide the answer to everyone's problems. The recordist who recorded the sync dialogue should also have recorded a background track of the atmosphere at the location where the dialogue scene was filmed – the factory noise–which you can use as a second soundtrack. When you go into the dubbing theatre with two separate tracks the sound mixer will be able to ensure that the sound levels of each track are as they should be – loud enough for the dialogue to stand out clearly above an audible but not deafening background.

Finding the right sounds

It is always best if wild tracks can be recorded at the locations at which scenes are filmed. Library recordings serve their purpose but the quality and variety of the sounds available on tape and disc do not compare to original sounds. It can be difficult to find the right noise for specific sound effects and it is easy to over-use a particular sound. I recall a young editor cutting a TV programme on the subject of world farming. The film had been shot in Europe, Asia and Australia but there was very little location sound: the editor relied on sound provided by one sound library. Like many television programmes, editing was done in a terrible rush and the editor used one open-country atmosphere track rather a lot. It was a very distinctive sound, recorded in England one day in spring. A lark and a few pigeons were very obvious and, because the track was used so much, in the finished film the same lark and pigeons appeared to follow the film unit round three continents! It all sounded absurd and the film had to be completely re-dubbed. The skilful use of sound in editing can be very satisfying but, if you are to do your job well, as with the picture master you must be presented with suitable raw materials to work with.

Identifying the take

When scenes are filmed it is important for the start and end of each scene to be clearly identified. You will rely on that identification when you start to cut, especially if the film has been shot with synchronized sound. The usual way of identifying sound and picture is to use a clapper board, which is usually referred to in the industry as a *slate*.

Before a sync sound scene is shot the director will ask the cameraman and the sound recordist to start their equipment. When the camera and the recorder have run up to speed someone will walk into shot with a clapper board. The title of the production and the cameraman's and director's names will be written across the top of the board, with the scene and take number down below. The person holding the board will read out the number of the scene and take and then create a sound 'clap' by raising and lowering a small hinged arm at the top of the board. 'Scene ten, take one,' he says as he bangs the two parts of the board together and moves out of shot. The director then calls for action. It's all over in a few seconds, but that board is very important. It identifies the production so if the film gets put on the wrong machine in a laboratory or anywhere else, anyone looking at the board will immediately be able to see the title of the production. Before you can start editing the film, or anyone can see and hear the results of the day's filming in sync, the sound and picture rushes must be synchronized: when you do that you will find the clapper board plays a key role, as we shall see later. When scenes are shot it is vital for the whole of the board to be seen, especially the top. It is equally important for the sound to be heard, and recorded, only after the recording equipment has run up to speed. If those basic rules are not observed you will find it difficult to synchronize sound and picture.

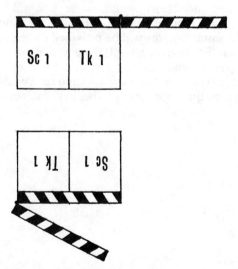

When identifying the start of a mute take, the clapper board should be held open. If unable to identify the start of a take, hold the clapper board upside-down at the end of it, banging it together if sound has been recorded.

So, in addition to your being provided with wild tracks and synchronized sound recordings, your job will be made much easier if every scene is clearly identified with a clapperboard at the start or end of each scene. There may be occasions where it is difficult to use a board. Perhaps someone forgot to take one to the location. That still does not mean the camera team cannot help you synchronize your material. As an emergency measure someone can write the scene and take number on a bit of paper, stand in front of the camera near a microphone and clap his hands together, simultaneously calling out the numbers written on the paper. If you can see the frame where the hands first meet and identify the clap on the recorded sound you will be able to sync up the scenes.

Identifying scenes without a slate

It is not always possible to identify the start of a scene, particularly when filming events which have not been staged for the film crew's benefit. A clapper board can, however, often be used at the end of the shot, but when that is done it should be held upside down. You will then know that the slate refers to the previous take and not spend hours trying to synchronize the wrong sound with the wrong track. Whenever possible a clapper board should be used for every shot. When there is no sound the top of the board should be held open so you will know the take is mute, not waste time looking for sound which has never existed.

There are some occasions when a clapper board cannot be used and where it is impractical to stand and clap hands in front of the camera. Filming a concert or some other scene where those taking part would be disturbed by any unnecessary noise is a typical example, but even in a situation like that the crew can still help you. If a microphone is filmed in close-up and tapped once clearly with a finger, you will be able to find the point where the finger touches the mike and identify it on the track. If the crew are efficient suitable notes will be provided on the camera and sound sheets to help you. 'Fanfare on arrival. Sync to end mike tap' is the sort of note you can expect to find.

So, with suitable sync sounds, wild tracks and clearly identified shots you can move into the cutting room ready to begin the job of editing sound and picture.

3

The cutting room

You will be working in a film cutting room. It will not be elaborate. There will probably be lino on the floor and plain painted walls which are easy to clean. The only interesting thing in a cutting room is the equipment in it, so let's see what you may find.

The sync bench

In one part of the room you will find a special kind of table. Hanging beneath it you will find two linen bags. The top of the surface of the table will have been cut away so that entry to the bags is unobstructed. Between the bags there may be a square glass panel about 18 inches wide. It will usually be of opal or frosted diffusing glass with a light located underneath it. On the extreme left-hand end of the table you will usually find a large, heavy, metal film *horse*. It consists of three or four sturdy metal poles about 18 inches high and ½ inch thick, permanently attached to a weighted metal base. A removable rod passes through divisions mid-way between

Take-up arm for right-hand end of synchronizer bench, showing hinged coupling on spindle, and spindle rest, which allows quick interchange of reels.

the top of the poles and the weighted base. A film horse is designed to hold several reels of film side by side at the same level. Separate reels of picture, picture and sound, or sound only are placed between the metal poles. The cross-bar passes through the centre of each reel. Film rotates when it is drawn off the reels and, as there is no obstruction, leaves the horse quite freely.

At the other end of the bench, to the right of the right-hand linen bag, you will probably find there is a geared *rewind arm* with a very long spindle. It is usually long enough to take four or five reels at a time. They are placed next to each other on the spindle, separated by small springs and held in position by a suitable clamp. Film coming from the film horse can be taken up on reels placed on this spindle without difficulty. Any slack film can be channelled into the linen bags. The table on which all these useful items are to be found is known as a '*sync bench*', or in some places as an *editing table*.

Synchronizers

The sync bench takes its name from a very important piece of equipment which you will normally find positioned mid-way between the two bags in the centre of the bench. It is called a *synchronizer*. It is one of the most important items in the room and you will find you use it at almost all stages of your work. In its simplest form (the *gang synchronizer*) a synchronizer consists of a series of large sprockets permanently fixed to a rotating shaft. Film is held on the sprockets by a series of sprung rollers which can be raised to place film on the sprocketed teeth and then lowered and locked to hold the film in position. The different sprockets on the synchronizer are fixed to a common drive shaft so they cannot be moved independently. If one sprocket turns the others move with it, so, if two pieces of film are placed in *level sync* ('*editorial sync*' in USA) they will remain synchronized whichever way the sprockets are turned.

The first sprocket, which will be nearest to you when you stand and face the bench, is normally used for picture. You will usually find that small magnetic soundheads are built into the other sprockets. These can be connected to a small amplifier and speaker and sound recorded on the various tracks placed on those sprockets can thus be heard. On some models the soundheads can be lowered so picture can be run on all the sprockets without scratching the film. When a synchronizer is used for matching master material it must not have soundheads for they will scratch any picture material run across them.

You are likely to use a synchronizer at various stages of cutting. As its purpose is to keep a number of different pieces of film in synchronization with each other it can be used for preserving sync between picture and separate magnetic soundtracks. It will also be used for matching the master material to the editing cutting copy. In the course of your work you will probably use a synchronizer with soundheads built into the second, third and fourth sprockets when you are cutting. When the camera master is matched to your edited cutting copy a synchronizer without soundheads will need to be used so that the master and the cutting copy can be run side

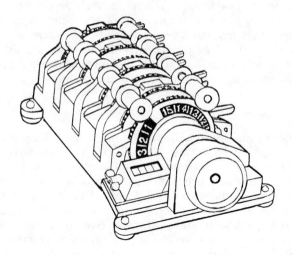

1

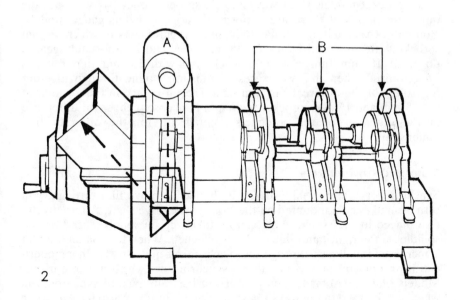

2

Synchronizers. 1, Four-way gang synchronizer, designed to hold four strips of film in synchronism. A footage or frame counter is standard equipment. 2, Four-way picture synchronizer. The picture in the front track is illuminated by a small lamp (A), which shines through the film via a prism to a small screen. The lamphouse can be moved so that you can mark the film. Small magnetic soundheads are frequently set into the other tracks (B).

by side without any risk of damage. When the synchronizer is placed above the illuminated glass panel in the middle of the bench light can shine through the film, thus making it possible to see the image on it and the edge numbers alongside. A *footage counter* is usually a standard fitting. It counts the footage as film passes through. It will work when film moves in either direction and it can be re-set to zero at any time.

Picture synchronizers

On many modern synchronizers there is a much more sophisticated and practical way of viewing the picture. A small screen is fitted above the front sprocket – the one which will be nearest you when you stand and face the bench. A lamp fitted a few inches above the sprocket shines through the film on to a prism set in the sprocket assembly. The prism back-projects a picture on to the screen. So that you can gain access to the film to mark your cutting points, the lamphouse is hinged. Synchronizers with integral screens are known as *picture synchronizers* or, more commonly in the parlance of the cutting room, as pic syncs. They are extremely useful and you should find a picture synchronizer in every well-equipped cutting room.

The number of sprockets on a synchronizer varies from model to model. Four-sprocket models (four-way) and six-sprocket ones (six-way) are the most common, but there are two-way versions and dual-gauge models. You will occasionally find dual 16/35 mm synchronizers in which 16 mm sprockets are mounted alongside 35 mm ones and appropriately geared down so 16 mm film placed in level sync with 35 mm film remains synchronized when the two pieces of film are wound through together regardless of the difference in film size. The difference in the location of the 35 mm and 16 mm sprocket teeth and the subsequent slight difference in the diameter of the sprockets compensate for the different film dimensions.

Motorized synchronizers

Synchronizers are normally driven by hand. To move film through, you turn a small handle mounted on the front of the drive shaft. Alternatively, film placed in the synchronizer can be taken up on spools placed on the spindle on the right-hand side of the sync bench. When tension on the film is increased it will pass through the synchronizer quite freely. In a modern cutting room you may come across synchronizers which are motorized. Models like the Acmade Competitor are basically picture synchronizers which can be used in the ways I have described, but they also have a motor attached to the rear of the sprocket assembly. It can be engaged to run film at a constant speed, or disengaged so you can move it freely. If you have a motorized editing machine in your cutting room a motorized pic sync is perhaps a luxury, but if there is no other way of running film at a constant speed it can fulfil an essential role. I generally edit on a Steenbeck but for a good many years have used a pic sync extensively and have done many basic jobs entirely on it. When motorized pic syncs were first introduced I thought they were an unnecessary luxury, but when I was later persuaded to buy one I was surprised how useful I found it. I still wind film through by hand most of the time but it is nice when you are cutting a sequence to be able to check it at a normal constant speed with several tracks, and a motorized picture synchronizer makes that possible. Now I would not want to be without it.

Equipment for cutting 16 mm with video

In the course of your work, as I have already mentioned, you may well find that at various stages you will be involved with video. If that is going to happen you will need suitable equipment in your cutting room, so let's briefly consider the various possibilities. You may need to synchronize 16 mm soundtracks to a video picture. That is not a problem. 16 mm synchronizers can be electronically locked to the output of a video recorder. With the right equipment installed, you can wind a video picture back and forth and expect 16 mm tracks in your film synchronizer to remain frame-accurately synchronized.

Motorized editing machines can likewise be locked to a video picture. You may perhaps wonder why anyone should ever want to use 16 mm soundtracks with a video picture. Is it not better to use the two tracks on the videocassette itself or mix in synchronism with a multi-track tape recorder? Again, costs have a bearing on how the job will be done. Video editing and dubbing time is expensive and it can take quite a long time to mix a detailed soundtrack and get a good result. 16 mm film dubbing is well proven, quite straightforward and very versatile. With practice you can put together a good soundtrack quite quickly. When you have dubbed your 16 mm tracks you can re-record the final mix on video. Producers working on restricted budgets, and those wishing to produce soundtracks with plenty of detail, often find they can get the best of both worlds by shooting on video, cutting the video picture and then fine-cutting with 16 mm soundtracks.

Intercutting film and video

I have just cut a production shot in four days on film and tape. The film was about the London Boat Show. Video cameras spent a day filming the exhibition. The sponsors also wanted to incorporate some shots of a power-boat race which had been shot earlier in the year on 16 mm film. I arranged for the 16 mm negative to be re-recorded on video and then intercut on U-Matic tape with the video recording of the exhibition. When I had finalized the picture assembly I arranged for the exhibition atmos- phere sound and an opening speech to be re-recorded from the tracks on the video to 16 mm film. Using my 16 mm pic sync locked electronically to a U-Matic video recorder I then built up a number of other soundtracks to bring the scenes to life. We then went into the dubbing theatre and recorded a commentary, again working on 16 mm film. That commentary and the other 16 mm tracks were then mixed together to make a final mix master 16 mm recording. Finally that master track was re-recorded on the original video film, replacing the original atmosphere tracks. Copies were distributed four days after the material had been shot and the whole job was completed with very little effort and at minimal cost.

Cutting a video picture with 16 mm sound

Producers working on shoestring budgets and shooting on video – and that includes many a student exercise – can also use 16 mm and video together, providing suitable equipment is available in the cutting room and the dubbing theatre. You will need a film picture synchronizer which can be run in synchronism with a video picture, and a motorized editing machine which can be locked in the same way. The dubbing theatre you intend to use must also be able to lock 16 mm tracks to a video picture. That will normally mean that the tape used must have a vertical-interval time code and a control track recorded on it. That can be done by the theatre or by a transfer studio or anyone else with a time-code generator and it should be done before you start to cut.

If you are asked to edit a production for someone who cannot afford broadcast-quality video equipment or a lot of video editing time you may well be able to improve the quality of the end result by working on 16 mm if the equipment I have described is available. For example, if you are asked to help with a film shot by students on low-band U-matic video, you will have a video picture with one or two video soundtracks as your raw material. It is perfectly possible to mix the two tracks on the tape together or do a basic dub on the tape itself with the use of discs or audio tapes to augment the video sound at suitable points, but the end result will not be very good and the effort involved may be considerable. The original video tracks could also be pre-mixed on another U-Matic video and then transferred back again, adding more sounds with each transfer, but working on a low-band tape like that and re-recording again and again you will not end up with sound which is very good quality. For a simple job that method of working may suffice but if you want to be creative and end up with a reasonably professional result you will find that two video sound tracks do not offer very exciting creative opportunities. To overcome that you can lift off the video sound in the way I described earlier and continue to work with the video picture. Alternatively you can telerecord the video picture on 16 mm film and cut the whole job on 16 mm film equipment. Telerecordings do not look particularly good but they are all right to work with. In the USA the term kinescope is widely used for telerecordings.

Take that low-band student video we have just considered, for example. Another way of editing it with 16 mm sound would be to telerecord the video picture on film, simultaneously re-recording the video soundtracks on 16 mm perforated magnetic film. Other tracks could then be added and edited with the telerecorded picture on a 16 mm pic sync or editing machine. When the programme has been fine-cut, the film can be dubbed and the final mix 16 mm soundtrack can be re-recorded alongside the edited video picture (which was fine-cut before you made a telerecording). When that has been done, the 16 mm telerecording, which has served its purpose, can be destroyed or filed away. The quality of the final sound track will be much better than it would be simply mixing and remixing the original tracks on low-band video.

A recap

Let's summarize. A synchronizer is essential for creative editing. It can be used to synchronize picture, as when matching master to a cutting copy, or picture to sound as you are editing. The picture can be on 16 mm film or on video. A synchronizer's job is to ensure that any film placed in level synchronization (editorial sync) on the sprockets remains in sync until the sprockets are opened and the film is removed. When the picture is on video synchronism between the tracks will be mechanical, as they are all located on the same drive shaft. The synchronizer itself will be electronically locked to the video signal by a special supplementary piece of equipment. Basic equipment consists of a series of sprockets locked to a common shaft which can be propelled by hand, driven by taking up the tension on slack film wound on to spools placed on the spindle on the right of the synchronizer, or by a small constant-speed motor. Footage and, some-times, frame counters are built in, as are individual volume controls for each soundhead on most up-to-date models. The first part of the synchro-nizer, nearest you when you face the bench, is normally used for picture, which is often projected on a small integral back-projection screen. The remaining sprockets are usually equipped with soundheads which can be used to replay sound when sprocketed magnetic film is wound through. The soundheads are connected to a separate amplifier and speaker.

Editing machines

The term 'editing machine' is much abused. To an amateur it can mean anything from a second-rate tape splicer, itself probably held together with tape, to some kind of animated viewer. As most amateurs seem to think a film editor simply cuts out the bad bits, perhaps that is not surprising. To a professional film-maker it means rather more, for you will find you rely on an editing machine to help you with your work. It will not do everything for you, like the machines found in many industrial manufacturing processes. One of the nice things about film editing is that the result depends on people and not machines. It is very much up to you, but if you have access to a well-designed editing machine you will find your work is easier to do. When you edit you will need to be able to view sound and picture together and independently at a variety of different speeds. Let's see what sort of equipment is available to help you.

One way of viewing picture is to use an *animated viewer*. Until a few years ago these were quite widely used by student film-makers and small film units and indeed you may still come across them, so let's consider how they work and what they will and will not do. Animated viewers consist of a few rollers, a picture gate and a small viewing screen, usually a few inches wide, rather like the screen on a picture synchronizer. The picture is projected by a rotating prism which operates when film passes through the rollers. Viewers are usually located on a baseboard with rewind arms on either side. There is no motor drive. To move film through a viewer you wind it from one rewind arm to the other via the viewer. The speed at which the film can be viewed depends entirely on the speed at which you

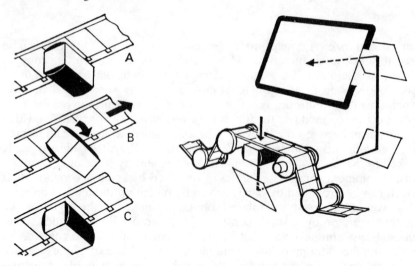

The viewer, where a picture is back-projected on a small screen via a rotating prism.

wind. For that reason it is almost impossible to assess the duration of any shot accurately, and viewers are thus not suitable for any sort of creative editing. If there is no other equipment available and you are editing very simple film which has been shot without sound, a viewer might be useful in the very first stages. You could assemble shots in the right order ready to be cut to length later on. A motorized editing machine could then be used to see the film at the speed at which the finished production will be projected. If you have to wind through several thousand feet of film looking for a particular scene or take and you do not have a picture synchronizer, an animated viewer may help. You can speed through what you do not want to use and slow down when you reach the vicinity of the shot required. In most cutting rooms, modern synchronizers have made animated viewers obsolete but from time to time you may still come across them, and for very basic assembly work when nothing else is available they can still serve a purpose.

Projectors in editing

Because animated viewers will not run at a constant speed and they will only run picture without separate soundtracks, they are not suitable for creative editing. *Projectors* are designed to run at a precise speed and there are some which will project picture with a separate magnetic soundtrack (*double-headed projection*). You may therefore think that a projector would be useful in editing. Unfortunately projectors are not much use in a cutting room. They are designed for constant running and not for stopping and starting and moving in all directions. No projector will stand the wear and tear involved in advanced editing and there is no projector capable of doing the jobs for which motorized editing machines are specially designed.

You will need an editing machine which is sturdily built. The picture gate must be accessible so you can mark your cutting points on the film with a wax pencil. Try and do that on a projector and you will find you have a problem. Most projector gates will open 45°. When you are cutting, a single frame can make all the difference. In a fast-moving action sequence one frame can make the difference between a good cut and a bad one. In a shot of a man running at speed, his right foot may be forward on one frame and level with his left foot on the next. To find the right cutting point you will need a machine which is accurate to one frame, one which can be stopped at precisely the right cutting point. A projector will not allow you to control the movement of the film accurately enough.

When to view

Although projectors are not designed for editing, at a few stages of the work they can play a useful part. They do not need to be in the cutting room. You can take the film along to a viewing theatre at those stages where constant-speed projection on a reasonable-size screen can be a help. It is nice to view rushes on a large screen and there is something to be said for projecting all rush prints before they are used on an editing machine. If there are technical problems you will be able to see them more clearly. Edge fogging, neg scratching and unsteadiness are all more obvious on a large screen. A few weeks ago I met a student film-maker who had produced a very good film. It was nicely shot and well put together. There was just one thing which spoiled the professionalism of the end product. About six shots in one sequence were edge fogged. I asked how that had happened and why he had decided to use those shots. Were no other takes available? He agreed that the fogging was unpleasant and said he was planning to re-cut the sequence using other takes as soon as he could raise the money to do so. He had not noticed the fogging before because he had only seen the cutting copy on an editing machine. The masking on the picture of the machine he was using was out of line so it cut off rather more of the right-hand side of the screen than it should have done. It was not a large amount but it was enough to hide that fogging, so it remained undetected until the first show copy was shown on a screen. By then it was too late. If the rushes had been projected on a screen before cutting began, the fault might have been noticed earlier. As it was, the student, who had otherwise done such an excellent job, had to meet all the costs involved in re-cutting that sequence, re-dubbing to insert new sound takes, re-cutting the master and making another print.

A projector can also be useful in the later stages of editing. I like to view a first assembly and a fine cut on a large screen. It makes it easier to gauge the pace of the film. When a film is projected without stopping you can see at a glance when a shot is longer or shorter than it should be, and that is how audiences will view the finished film. So, projectors can have a part to play in editing; but for the actual work of cutting scenes together you will need a specially designed motorized editing machine.

Multi-speed machine

An editing machine must show a picture of reasonable quality. That picture needs to be clear, reasonably steady and large enough for you to be able to see details like footsteps and lip movements, all of which can be crucial when you are cutting with sound. It should be able to run at various speeds. Normal sound-projection speed and a fast speed are basic essentials, and you will find most modern editing machines will run at 24 frames per second or 25 fps and at double speed or even faster. 24 fps is the standard sound-projection speed for cinemas and projectors used in schools, universities and other non-theatic locations. Most television stations project their films on telecine machines running at 25 fps. The average member of the public probably would not notice the difference, but with practice you will, particularly when you have heard the same sound time and time again. You do not need to worry too much about what speed you cut at as one frame will not make much difference to how you assess your cutting points, but if you are recording or transferring sound, particularly a commentary, you must ensure you record at the speed at which the final film will be projected. If you are cutting a television programme shot on location at 25 fps and go into a dubbing theatre and record links of voice-over narration at 24 fps, the finished track will sound wrong. If you project it at 25 fps the commentary will sound fast. If you run it at 24 fps the location sound will be slow. So you must know from the outset what speed the film has been shot at and what it is going to be used for at the end of the day.

Your editing machine should also run at double speed, or, preferably, even faster. You will find that a great advantage, for while your cutting copy may be very enjoyable the first hundred times you see it, when you have run through the whole thing from the beginning time after time and want to make an adjustment some way from the head of the reel, you will welcome a way of getting to it quickly. A machine which can speed through shots you are not immediately concerned with will save time, money and hours of frustration.

So you will need an editing machine which will run picture at normal speed and faster with acceptable standards of picture illumination and steadiness. It will also need to run one or more separate soundtracks recorded on perforated magnetic film. Most professional editing machines run a 16 mm picture with one or two 16 mm tracks. You may sometimes find you come across machines which will run a 16 mm picture and 35 mm tracks. There are still some 16/35 mm editing machines around. They were used quite a lot when 16 mm was first used for professional productions. In those days very few dubbing theatres could run 16 mm soundtracks. Rather than re-equip everything they put in 16 mm projectors which would run in sync with 35 mm tracks. Editing equipment manufacturers cashed in and enthusiasts pointed out that the quality of a 35 mm mag track is better than a 16 mm one. That is still true but nowadays, while there are still a few 16/35 editing machines around and still some dubbing theatres which can run a 16 mm picture with 35 mm sound, there are many more which handle 16 mm and video exclusively.

Choosing an editing machine

There are a number of different types of motorized editing machine designed to handle the simultaneous editing of sound and picture. Some are quite cheap while others are expensive. Why is there such a difference in price between machines designed to do a similar job? Take a closer look, or better still cut a film on them, and you will soon spot the difference. Most cut-price machines are unpleasant to use. They can make the simplest job seem complex. Too many low-cost machines are built down to a price instead of up to a realistic specification.

There are two types of machine in wide professional use and they are types you will find you can trust. There are upright machines, like the Moviola, and table models, like the Steenbeck. In the great days of Hollywood, upright machines like the Moviola were used everywhere. Indeed they became so common that the brand-name Moviola was often used to mean an editing machine and it still is today in many places, though if one is strictly accurate about it a Moviola is a machine made by one very experienced manufacturer. Today many editors prefer to use table models like the Steenbeck, and the Moviola Company has brought out its own table models. For 16 mm work I find table models are ideal, but there are editors who prefer to use the older designs, and many upright Moviolas are still in use in cutting rooms. They are both good types of equipment and all editors have their personal preferences, as you will when you have worked with a number of different models.

Upright machines

Upright Moviolas are ideal for handling short lengths of film. The picture is driven by an intermittent sprocket with loops above and below the picture gate. There is a small, bright picture and the machine can be controlled by hand or a foot pedal. Sound and picture can be run together in sync or independently. Upright Moviolas are ideal for running individual film shots. When working with reels of film I personally prefer to use a table model.

Editing tables

On a fairly typical table editing machine like the Steenbeck 1601, picture and sound pass from left to right horizontally across what is basically a flat table. You sit in front. When you use a table machine you will wind your film on plastic cores instead of reels. The cores rest on metal plates, two on the feed side to the left of the picture gate and soundhead, and two on the right, for take-up. On the 1601, which is designed to handle one reel of picture and one soundtrack, the picture runs farthest away from you. It passes round a series of sprockets and rollers and is back-projected by a high-quality rotating prism on to an eye-level screen. Running parallel with the picture but immediately in front of you there is one track of magnetic sound. The sound is fed to a speaker on the right of the screen. Movement through the machine is controlled by a small lever immediately in front of

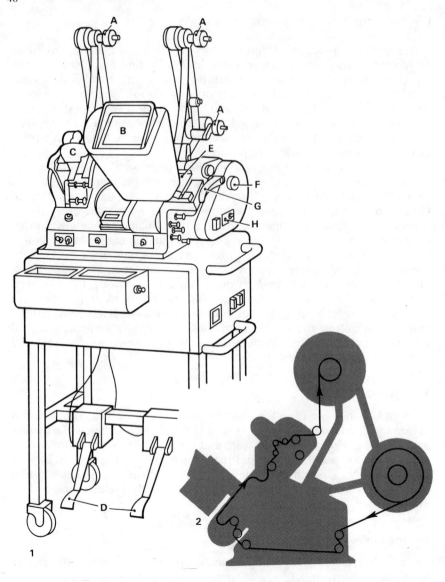

The Hollywood Moviola. 1, Layout and controls. Film passes from feed spindles (A) to take-up, with sound running on the left via the soundhead (C) and picture on the right, where it is projected on a screen (B). The screen can be moved to give access to the film by releasing the locking catch (E). A brake for instant stopping (G), picture and motor on/off switches (H) and a picture-head motor rheostat control are all on the right. Film speed direction and control pedals are below the machine (D). 2, Film lacing path. Picture film passes from top to bottom via two feed sprockets and a loop (of nine or ten frames) to the picture gate. Another loop of nine or ten frames after the picture gate leads the film via a further feed sprocket to the take-up.

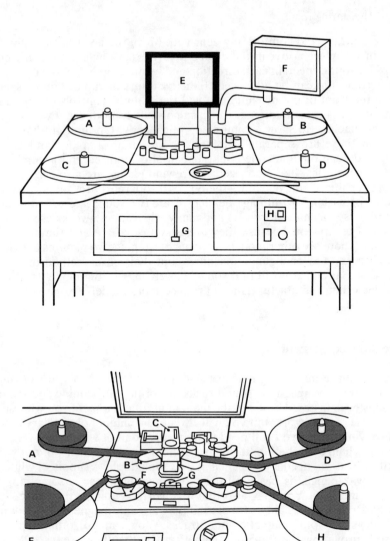

Steenbeck editing table. 1, 16 mm four-plate model. The picture feed plate (A) and take-up plate (B), and the sound feed plate (C) and take-up plate (D), are set above the main on/off controls (H) and a volume control (G). The picture is back-projected on an eye-level screen (E) with a loudspeaker alongside (F). 2, Lacing path and direction control. Picture (A) passes via a drive sprocket (B) through the picture gate (C), where a rotating prism back-projects on the screen above, and then on to the picture take-up plate (D). Magnetic sound (E) passes via a drive sprocket (F) over the magnetic sound head (G) to the take-up (H). One lever (J) operates variable-speed forward and reverse direction controls.

the soundtrack and comfortably near you. Move the lever to the right and the film advances. Move it to the left and it runs back again. There are click stops for sound speed in each direction and by moving the handle less far or further the film can be advanced frame by frame or run at double speed.

On the front of the machine you will find volume controls for the track and for an optical soundtrack, which can also be reproduced if you want to use the machine to show a combined optical copy. On the right-hand side in front there are separate switches for the lamp, amplifer and exciter lamp. Footage or time-code counters can also be fitted and a number of useful accessories, like motorized fast rewind plates, are also available. A larger version of this machine–the ST 1901–operates in a similar manner but has provision for running one picture and two soundtracks. I have used one of these machines for years and many television networks use them as standard equipment because they are easy to operate and they are very reliable. There are other models, capable of running two pictures and more soundtracks, and dual-gauge machines, but their basic method of operation is similar and you will find you can easily move from model to model. Various other manufacturers also produce table models designed to do a similar job.

Ancillary equipment

You now have an editing machine and a synchronizer, so you can run a cutting copy and magnetic soundtracks at normal and double speeds and perhaps even faster. Those are the main items of equipment you will use in the course of your work, but you will also need a number of ancillary items. Before you can cut you will need to mark the point at which you want the scene to change on the film itself. An ordinary pen or pencil will not write on film. You will need a wax pencil like a Chinagraph. A supply of white or yellow wax pencils is basic cutting-room equipment, as is something to keep them sharp. You may also find it is worth keeping a pair of scissors handy. Brass scissors are best because they are anti-magnetic and will not put clicks on your magnetic soundtracks. You can use other types of scissors providing they are de-magnetized before they are used to cut tracks. When you have marked your cutting points the film can be cut and joined and to do that you will need a *film splicer*.

Film splicers

There are two main ways of joining film – with a liquid solution called film cement or with transparent tape. Both are used in the course of editing any professional film. *Tape joins* are normally used for cutting-copy action and sound and cement for master materials. When a *cement splice* is made film is cut and the emulsion is scraped off a small part of one frame on one side of the splice. Cement is applied to the clear film and the shot to be joined to it is brought in contact with the cement-coated clear edge before it has time to dry and harden. The second piece of film is not scraped clear. If it was light would pass straight through the resulting clear strip and a white

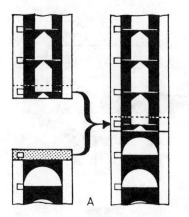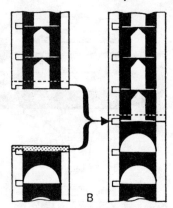

When splicing 16 mm film with a cement splice a small overlap (B) is preferable when slicing most materials. The larger overlap (A) will give added strength to a splice, but will also appear more obvious when the film is projected.

flash would appear on the screen. The second piece of film is however cut to a slightly different length to allow for the overlap. The two pieces of film are thus virtually welded together.

Joining with tape

When a tape splicer is used the procedure is quite different. When you join with tape you do not need an overlap when you make the cut. Just cut and lay the two pieces of film end to end so they touch each other but do not overlap. A piece of transparent adhesive tape can then be drawn across both pieces of film, and the sprocket holes can be punched clear of tape. You do not need cement, or patience, because you do not have to wait for cement to dry. The join is completed in seconds but beware! Remember that though you do not need to overlap the film when you join your cutting copy with tape, when you have completed your work and the master is matched to it, the negative cutter who will do the matching for you will need extra frames to make a cement splice, so before you make your cuts check to ensure those frames will be available.

Cement or tape?

Both systems have advantages and disadvantages. As frames are lost when splices are made with cement it can be difficult to change a cut. You have to determine how many frames are missing by calculating the distance between the edge numbers and insert spacing to length to build up the shots. If you have joined with tape and want to alter a cut you will not have any problems. Just peel the join and replace any section you wish to place or cut elsewhere as you wish. If you do replace sections check the edge numbers just to make sure you have not accidentally lost any frames. It is all quite simple and that is why it is best to use tape when you are working with a cutting copy and cement splices for anything else.

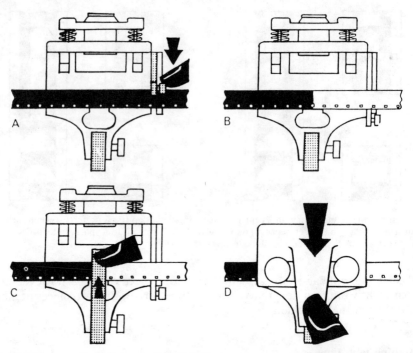

Stages in the operation of a tape splicer. (A) Place one piece of film across splicer, with the point at which you wish to cut on the right-hand edge, and bring knife down to cut it. (B) Move pieces of film you wish to splice to the centre of the splicer. (C) Cover both pieces with tape. (D) Bring down top of splicer to cut tape and clear sprocket holes.

Cement splices are essential for master materials. If you have to repair a damaged show print, join on a new leader or make a cut anywhere in the film, a cement splice will be the best one to use on that occasion too. Tape splices are thicker than cement ones and some projectors do not like them. Cement joins can be almost invisible when projected, especially when film is joined in A and B rolls, as we shall see later. Tape splices are always visible because the tape must cover two or more frames and, although it is transparent, as time passes it discolours. For joining magnetic soundtracks tape splices are unbeatable. You can join straight or diagonally and tape will work admirably.

Whichever type of join you use always make sure you use good-quality materials. Choose a tape made for the purpose. Remember that as the tape has to pass through delicate editing equipment time after time it must be strong and thin. It is no good trying to use the tape you employ to tie up your parcels. When you complete a tape splice, check the edges of the film and the perforations. Is the cut cleanly trimmed or are there loose bits of tape on the edges of the film or clogging the sprocket holes? If there are it is probably because the cutting blades in the joiner you are using are blunt, out of line or themselves clogged with film or tape trims. Always use tape on the cellulose (shiny) side of the film or soundtrack and not on the emulsion. If you are using cement make sure it is fresh. It does not keep for ever. In a large studio cement is changed every morning. Keep the splicer clean and always put the lid back on the cement bottle immediately after you have used it. That will prevent air shortening the life of any cement left in the bottle.

Cement splicers

There are several different types of cement splicers. In some cutting rooms, particularly those in the older, well-established major studios, you will probably find a foot-pedal-operated one which can be used for 35 mm and 16 mm film. These joiners make the most durable splices and with very little practice they are easy to use. When I first started in the cutting rooms, tape joiners were a rarity and everything had to be joined with cement. The editor made his cuts on an editing machine or synchronizer and then wound the film on to a reel with the scenes to be joined held together with

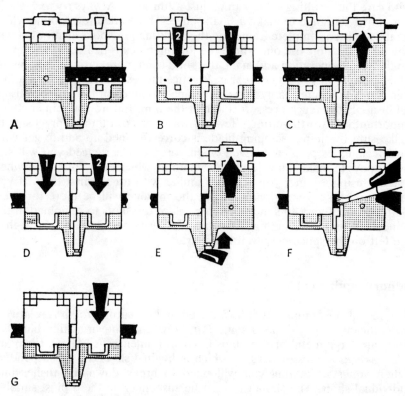

Stages in the operation of a cement splicer. (A) Place one piece of film on right-hand side of splicer. (B) Lower top of right-hand side and bring left-hand side down to cut the film opposite. (C) Raise right-hand side again and insert film on left side. (D) Bring right-hand side down again to cut film on left. (E) Raise right-hand side and scrape piece of left side still visible. (F) Apply cement to left-side portion. (G) Bring right side down in contact with wet cement. Wait 10 secs., release both sides and inspect.

paper sleeves or clips. As each reel was assembled it was passed to the trainee assistant editor, who spent much of his time at the foot joiner. It's not a bad way to learn how to handle film. Nowadays tape splicers have eliminated all that and editors make their own joins, but you may still come across a foot joiner from time to time.

A more common kind of cement splicer, which is much more portable, is the Robot. It incorporates an automatic splicer. Simply place the two scenes you want to join on two sets of teeth end to end. One operation cuts the film to length. Another scrapes the emulsion off one side and the two pieces of film are then brought in contact with each other. The job is completed in a matter of seconds. Cement is put on the film by a small rotating wheel which is immersed in a well of cement. You do not have to scrape the film or apply cement with a brush. The machine takes care of the whole operation. It's robotic. You just use two handles to control the various operations.

There are also a number of much smaller splicers made by various manufacturers. They may take a few seconds longer to make a splice than a foot joiner or the Robot I have described above, but if the join is made with care the resulting splice can be just as durable. Always try to use a 16 mm joiner designed to make a small splice. There are a few around which scrape almost a complete frame and the resulting join looks awful whatever you do. If possible use one where the joining block is heated. It will speed up the whole operation and make the bond even more durable. Scrape the film carefully so you do not tear it. Practice makes perfect. When you first join film you will probably find you scrape too much or too little emulsion off or apply too much pressure and tear the film. Before you join anything important it is worth getting a few old waste bits of film and practising to make sure the joiner scraping blade is correctly lined up and to get your own techniques perfected. Even when you are experienced you will still find it pays to make a few joins on something which does not matter when you are using a joiner you are not familiar with for the first time. If you make a mistake joining with cement the mistake will be there for ever. Before you attempt to splice anything, place the shots to be joined in the joiner, cut them to length and clean off any wax pencil marks, for if they are left on the splice may well fall apart.

Sundry equipment

The rest of the equipment you will need in your cutting room is relatively insignificant. You will need some *film bins* (also known as film barrels). They are large metal or fibre bins lined with linen bags. Above them are *editing racks* – clips or pegs on which individual shots can be suspended. When you start editing you will need to break down the rushes into individual shots. The shots can then be suspended in these bins, suitably identified with wax pencil marks written on the film and on top of the peg or clip. When you have made your cut the part of the shot you are taking out and not using (the trim) can be returned to the bin, hence the name 'trims bin'. You will also need a waste bin for throwing away any film not required.

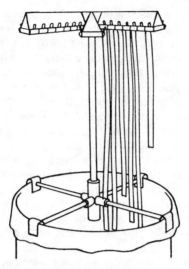

The trim bin. Shots are sorted into order and held by numbered clips on the cross bars. Other ends hang inside the linen bag, which prevents damage.

Flat rewinds

In some cutting rooms you may also find a *flat rewind table*. It is made up of two large plates for holding film, possibly set on either side of a small illuminated inspection panel. It is called a flat rewind because the plates on which film is laid on cores are horizontal and not vertical. Flat rewinds are useful for examining film or for quickly rewinding large reels. To move film in each direction you usually have to turn a small handle built into the front of the table, but there are some more expensive models which are motorized. The speed at which the film is taken up can be controlled by the amount of pressure applied to a foot pedal. Again if you are not used to the equipment you will find it pays to experiment before you rewind any valuable film. You might think flat rewinds were foolproof, and with a little practice they are, for they are really very simple, but that does not mean mistakes cannot be made. I remember one particularly unfortunate incident which occurred in a cutting room of a London-based television company. A 35 mm film copy of an American TV programme had been flown in that morning from the USA and an editor had spent several hours editing out the American commercials ready for the programme to be broadcast on English television that same day. The programme ran for thirty minutes – that is 3,000 ft of 35 mm film, which can be quite a weight to handle. When the editor had made his cuts he passed the film to his assistant to rewind. The assistant decided to use a flat rewind table which had recently been installed in the cutting room. He placed the film on the plates and depressed a foot pedal to start the rewind. For the first minute everything went well; then the film gained momentum. As the take-up plate got fuller the film started to move at a considerable speed. The assistant soon realized it was going too fast but, as he was not familiar with the equipment, he was not sure how to stop it. If he pressed the stop pedal he thought the plates might stop abruptly and snap the film. As he was only too well aware that the print he was handling was the only copy in the country, due to be transmitted to an estimated audience of ten million people that very night, he realized that he was in trouble and turned to ask his editor what he should do. Unfortunately the editor had just left the room. The assistant could hear his voice along the corridor, so he stood up and ran to the doorway to get some help, leaving the film running faster and faster on the flat rewind. As he reached the door and started to call for help the film shot off the take-up plate and flew out of a nearby window. It was subsequently recovered from the car park down below. It was a day no one in that cutting room will ever forget. So, make sure you know how the equipment you are going to use works. Read the instructions if they are available or watch and ask people who have more experience. Never be afraid to ask about anything. That is the best way to learn.

A series of racks to hold cans of film and reels of a few basic materials will complete the main equipment you will need in your cutting room. White spacing, leaders, clear film and black-framed opaque film (known as *black masked buzz*) will all be needed. Spare rolls of joining tape, a ruler to draw straight lines with your wax pencils and some clean linen gloves in case you have to handle any master material will also be useful. It is also worth making sure you have spare lamps for the picture synchronizer and your editing machine so if one blows you will not waste time waiting for a replacement.

Cutting-room layout

You now know a little bit more about the equipment you are going to have to use in the course of your work. The way in which that equipment is laid out is also worth a few minutes' thought. The important thing is to make everything accessible and to keep the items you will use most near to each other so you will not have to waste time moving all over the place and there will be no need to drag lengths of film right across the room. You should not need to look under anything or stand on a chair every time you need a can of film. Make sure that if possible the light from any window in the cutting room shines sideways across the editing machine and does not come from in front or behind it. If it is behind you a bright light may make any picture difficult to see. If you are facing it you may find it is tiring and hard to concentrate and have to work all day with the blinds down. Let us consider two possible layouts.

You could put your sync bench by the window and alongside it the trims bin. That bin may well be on wheels so you can move it around. If it is you will find that is very helpful. On the right-hand wall of the room, at right angles to the sync bench, you could put the editing machine, and on the right of that there is room for a splicer. If you lay out the room like that you have immediately established a kind of production line. The editing machine and the sync bench are conveniently near each other. If you want to make a cement splice the joiner is also nearby so you will not have to drag film all over the floor. For most of your work you will probably be using a tape joiner which can be used on the editing machine, the sync bench or on any convenient flat surface. Against the wall opposite the editing machine there is room for some film racks and a flat rewind. If you have an animated viewer it could go on a table next to the rewind or alternatively that table could be used for paperwork. Chairs in front of the table and the editing machine, together with a high stool in front of the sync bench, will complete the picture.

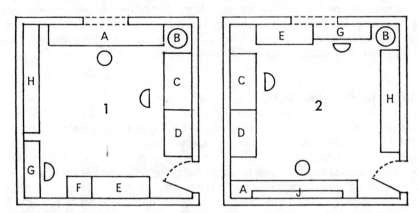

Cutting-room layouts. (A) Sync bench (under window). (B) Trim bin. (C) Editing machine. (D) Splicer. (E) Viewer. (F) Table. (G) Flat rewind. (H) Racks. (J) Trim bin attached to wall.

Another way of laying out the cutting room would be to place the table with the viewer and the flat rewind table in the window and have the sync bench alongside the opposite wall. You could use a mobile trims bin or have one fixed to the wall behind the bench, or opt for both. Any cement splicer could be kept at the end of the sync bench and alongside, occupying another wall, the editing machine. That leaves a wall free for racks and a waste bin. In both the arrangements I have described everything you will need to get at is accessible and the two items you will use most – the editing machine and the sync bench – are in easy reach of each other. If the layout of a cutting room is carefully considered it will save time and make your job easier.

Cutting-room hire

Well-equipped cutting rooms can be hired by the day, the week or the month. The main items you will need can also be hired for use on your premises from specialist rental companies, but you will probably find it is best to hire a complete cutting room if you do not have enough regular work to justify setting up your own. Don't risk ruining a potentially good film by trying to be creative with the wrong equipment. An animated viewer and a pair of rewind arms should not be used simply because nothing else is available. If you do not have the right equipment to do the job properly, hire it. If you are on a really tight budget you may be able to use a sync bench and a picture synchronizer, and possibly rent a motorized editing machine to finish the job.

When you hire a cutting room make sure it has the right equipment for the sort of film you are going to cut. Is it the right gauge? Is it up to date and in good working order or has it been used for years without adequate maintenance? Does whoever is hiring you the cutting room agree to carry out any repairs if equipment breaks down, or will the cost be passed on to you? You should expect to meet the cost of any raw materials you use like joining tape, spacing and leader but it is worth finding out how the charges will be assessed before you move in. If a telephone is installed how much are you going to have to pay to use it? On the face of it they are all small points but they can add up and give you a nasty surprise.

Hiring preview theatres

In the course of your work you may need to hire other facilities. Viewing and dubbing theatres will be needed and you may want someone to shoot titles on a rostrum camera, unless you are going to complete your production on video. Preview theatres can be hired on an hourly basis. The charge made usually includes the services of a projectionist. Again make sure the theatre you hire can show the type of film you want to project. If you want to show a cutting copy with a separate soundtrack explain that you want a 16 mm double-head projector capable of running a mute picture with a separate magnetic soundtrack. You will find many theatres can run double-headed but most of them can only run one track. If you want to project your picture with more than one track you will need to hire a dubbing theatre and that will be much more expensive. You should also specify the speed you want the film projected at – 24 or 25 fps. If you hve a combined print make sure the theatre can show a comopt print or a commag one depending on what it is you wish to show. If you check before you book you can save yourself a lot of trouble. If time permits, especially if you are intending to show the film to other people, it is worth writing to confirm the booking. Put the date, time and your exact requirements on paper and say how long you want the facilities for and you are less likely to find yourself in the embarrassing position of arriving and finding your telephone reservation has been forgotten and someone else has arrived for the same time slot.

Dubbing-theatre hire

When you complete your cutting you will need to go into a dubbing theatre for the final stage of mixing together the soundtracks you have prepared. Dubbing theatres are quite expensive so you need to carefully assess the amount of time you book a theatre for. That will depend on the number of tracks you have to mix, how complicated and how efficiently prepared they are, and on how well equipped and efficient the dubbing theatre is. There can be no hard and fast rules, for time requirements can differ considerably from job to job but, if you want to end up with a good track, it is important not to underestimate the time required. If you have a simple thirty-minute film with two tracks of reasonably straightforward effects well matched to the picture and a reel of commentary, an hour and a half may well suffice. If the quality of the tracks is poor more time will be needed to try to improve them. If they are out of sync or inefficiently laid more time will be wasted. If your joins fall apart you will have to start again and the bill will go up once more, but those are all points which can be anticipated.

If you have five tracks of sound effects, two of music and three of dialogue, a half-hour film could take half a day or more to mix. If you are doubtful about the time you need ask the dubbing theatre sound mixer to advise you. He is the person who will actually do the job. Tell him what tracks you are going to be bringing into his theatre and ask his advice. That is far better than guessing yourself and ending up with a half-finished film at the end of the time you have booked in the theatre and another editor waiting to come in.

When you hire a dubbing theatre you hire a complete package of staff and equipment. You will have the services of a sound mixer and one or more assistants. They will lace up your edited soundtracks on machines which will replay them and load a reel of new magnetic stock on to a recording machine locked to run in sync with your tracks and the picture. A projectionist completes the dubbing theatre crew, though nowadays in many dubbing theatres projection work is done by one of the sound assistants. Your cutting copy will be laced up on a projector or projected on a TV screen via a video camera. If you are mixing 16 mm tracks to a video picture a cassette copy of the programme will be used to provide the picture. The hourly charge made for the theatre covers everything usually, including the most welcome facility of all – endless cups of coffee.

One important point to check when you book a dubbing theatre is the number of tracks they can run at any one time. How many tracks can they project in sync with your edited picture? It is two or ten? If they can only run two and you have six tracks, the film will have to be run through several times. On the first run two tracks can be mixed, on the second one more can be added, and so on. It will take a long time and each re-mix will take your soundtrack another stage away from the original sound. In a large theatre capable of running a number of tracks simultaneously they can run all your tracks at once, though the sound mixer may not wish to do so. It is quite normal to mix together any dialogue and then go through again adding music and sound effects. That may sound a waste of time, but you will find it isn't. If the mixer mixes the sound effects together and then adds the music he will know exactly how loud the effects need to be at each point and he can get the balance right, calculating his fades and sound levels accordingly. This system of mixing tracks bit by bit is known as *pre-mixing*.

When you book a dubbing theatre it is, of course, essential to ascertain which gauge of soundtrack they are equipped to handle. If you are cutting a 16 mm film with 16 mm tracks check that they can run them satisfactorily. If you are synchronizing tracks to a video picture make sure the theatre can lock 16 mm sound to your low-band U-Matic tape or whatever it is you intend to use. There are still a few dubbing theatres which can only run a 16 mm picture with 35 mm tracks, and quite a number which will not handle

16 mm at all because they specialize in dubbing features. So, check before you book. You will soon find you get to know which dubbing theatres are good and which are not so efficient. A great deal will depend on the ability of the sound mixer. It's a skilled job and one where experience pays dividends. Anyone can learn the basic mechanics of sound mixing but in my experience really good mixers have a feel for the job which is innate. The more efficient the person in charge is the better the job will be and the more quickly it will be completed. When you have found a good dubbing theatre you will probably want to use it regularly. A mixer gets used to working with an editor and it helps if each understands the other's problems and objectives.

Efficiency also depends on you. Do not expect to get good results from poorly prepared tracks. It is important to ensure that before you go into a dub you have tracks which are of a professional standard. Do not expect miracles if you arrive with tracks which are out of sync or incomplete. The sound mixer may be able to redeem something but if he is going to produce a good-quality dub you must give him good materials to work with. You will find it pays to check all your tracks carefully in the cutting room before you set out for the dubbing theatre. If one track is out of sync you can correct the error much more easily and cheaply in the cutting room than you can in a dubbing theatre. It also pays to ensure that you have all the sounds you need on your soundtracks. If a few sounds are missing it may be possible to add them from loops, tapes or discs in the course of a dub, but that should be regarded as an emergency measure. Working like that will slow the whole operation down. It may not be possible to find the right sounds or difficult to match them to the picture. It is bound to take time, and dubbing time is expensive. So, before you go off to dub make sure the tracks you have prepared are complete and in sync, with start marks clearly visible on the start of each roll and plenty of spare leader to lace up the machines with. Check all the joins so they will not fall apart. If they do you will have to go back to the start of the reel. They are all small points but they can save a lot of money–and anger.

Titling facilities

You may also need to hire a specialist to help you with titles. Because titles superimposed on film tend to be expensive, many 16 mm productions not intended for showing on film screens are now titled on video. If the production you are cutting is only going to be shown on television or video it is quite possible to complete your cutting and make a show print incorporating the title background and then add the title lettering electronically on video. The alternative is to shoot the titles on film and superimpose them in a more conventional way. If you decide to do that you may need the services of a titling studio. Again it pays to choose carefully. It is a good idea to see examples of the work the studio has produced if you are not familiar with it already. Make sure they show you examples of work completed on a similar budget. There is no point in looking at wonderful 70 mm title sequences when you are looking for a studio to produce a simple title for a low-budget 16 mm documentary.They may be the best title makers in the world for prestige productions and have no interest at all in 16 mm. When you find a studio with suitable equipment and enthusiasm they will be able to draw the titles for you and shoot them on a special rostrum camera. You will have to arrange for them to be married up with the appropriate backgrounds: we shall see how that can be done later. The normal procedure when commissioning title work is to pay for each title or diagram. The studio will give you a quotation for preparing each title. The figure will cover the cost of drawing a title card and a cameraman's time shooting the card on a special rostrum camera and the film stock required. The cost of processing may or may not be included and you should always ask if the figure quoted includes processing the master and supplying a cutting print. We shall be exploring the techniques you will have to use to put titles on your film in more detail in a later chapter.

4

The mechanics of editing visuals

Editing time

How long will it take you to edit your film? It's a difficult question to answer, for the answer depends on a number of different factors. How long is the finished film supposed to be? How much material have you got to work with? How complicated is the work likely to be? A fifteen-minute film can be cut in a day if it simply consists of sync sound interviews – or talking heads, as they are usually referred to in the trade. On the other hand, if a film crew has been all over the place shooting thousands of feet of film and numerous wild tracks it could take several weeks to cut a film running for the same time. As you gain experience you will find you get quicker but there are some stages of the job which it is difficult to rush. If you work in television you may well find you are sometimes working against the clock. The introduction of video has meant that many rush jobs are now done on tape and not film. Television news, for example, is usually transmitted live with video inserts, but film is still used for less topical reports. When I first worked in television video did not exist. Some programmes were tele-recorded on film but many were transmitted live or shot on film in the first place. All the sports programmes, for example, were filmed during the afternoon, taken by despatch riders to the laboratory, processed and brought back to us in the cutting rooms. We then cut the master, which was transmitted the same night. If we made a mistake millions of people saw it, and plenty were made, I can assure you! I can vividly recall a night when one of the joins in a topical magazine programme I had cut fell apart as it was being televised. Fortunately the join broke after the projector gate so the film remained in sync. Miraculously it continued to run through but it could not be rewound on the take-up spool. For half an hour a small army of people shovelled the film into bins as it rolled off the telecine projector, and ten million viewers at home remained blissfully unaware of what was going on.

The main stages of editing

There are still some programmes where you may find you have to meet very tight deadlines, but for most of your work you should be able to organize a timetable to suit the needs of the subject you are working on. The work of editing a film can be broken down into ten main stages. Let's see what they are.

1. **Shoot and process** the camera original (the master film)
2. **Make a rush print** for editing (the cutting copy). In the USA 'rushes' are often called 'dailies'.
3. **Synchronize sound and picture rushes** so they can be viewed and the best takes selected.
4. **Log rushes**, noting edge numbers and a brief summary of the content of each scene. If you have to replace a damaged shot or need to find a scene in a hurry when cutting is underway you will find it is easier if you have first logged the rushes.
5. **Break down rushes** into individual shots and hang them in a bin, or if they are very long takes wind them into individual rolls held in place with an elastic band.
6. **Make first assembly**. Assemble shots in the right order.
7. **Fine cut**. To give the film a variety of pace and make it interesting to watch.
8. **Prepare soundtracks** edited to match the fine-cut action.
9. **Dub**. Mix all the individual tracks of music, sound effects and dialogue together to produce a final mix master recording.
10. **Neg cut and produce show prints**. The master film can be matched to your edited cutting copy and an answer print and show copies can be ordered from the laboratory.

Synchronizing rushes

When the film first arrives in your cutting room it will come in at least two separate cans – one of sound and one of picture. Before the rushes can be viewed you will have to synchronize the mute reel(s) of picture with the sound recorded on perforated magnetic film. You will need a synchronizer complete with an amplifer. You will also need a film horse and two spools on which to take up the synchronized rushes together with a splicer to rejoin them ready for projection. Begin by taking the first reel of picture and putting it in the first track of the film horse. That is the one nearest you as you face the sync bench. Put the first reel of magnetic sound next to it. Make sure it leaves the horse with the emulsion side (the dull one) facing the soundheads built into the synchronizer. On most modern synchronizers the soundheads are built into the sprockets so the emulsion side of the track should face downwards. If you should find yourself using one of the old type of synchronizers with detachable soundheads mounted on top, the emulsion should be other way round, so again it faces the soundheads.

Place the magnetic film on the teeth of the second track of the synchronizer and lock it in position. Now, adjust the volume of the track reader and move the magnetic film across the soundhead. You should soon hear evidence of a recording. Now is the time to refer to the sound recordist's information sheets and to the camera sheets provided by the cameraman and to any additional information which may or may not have been provided by a continuity secretary. See what this reel should contain and then you will know what to look for. After winding through a few feet you should hear a voice identifying the first take. It will simply state the scene or take number, and will be followed by a bang on the track. This bang is, of course, the noise of the two parts of the clapper board coming in contact with each other. Wind the track very slowly and carefully over the magnetic head in the synchronizer and mark with a cross the exact point where the bang starts, filling one frame and no more. Alongside your mark, write the scene and take number with a wax pencil.

Now you can look at the picture. Somewhere you will find a series of frames picturing the clapper board with the same scene and take number as you have just heard on the track. Look at it carefully and find the exact point in the action where the two sections of the clapper board first meet. Mark that frame with a cross and the scene and take numbers. Open the synchronizer again and put your two marks opposite each other. Sound and picture are now synchronized.

To be more precise they are in 'level synchronization', or level sync, as everyone says in a cutting room. Now you can splice some white spacing film on the sound and picture, taking care to splice on the right-hand side of the synchronizer. When that has been attached, wind back and put a large start mark on both pieces of film at the same point. A start mark takes the form of a large cross on the picture and three straight lines or a large cross on the soundtrack. It should occupy only one frame. At the head of both rolls mark the title of the film and the fact that this is reel one, then place the ends of the spacing in take-up spools and wind on. As the wax pencil marks identifying the position of the clapper board pass through

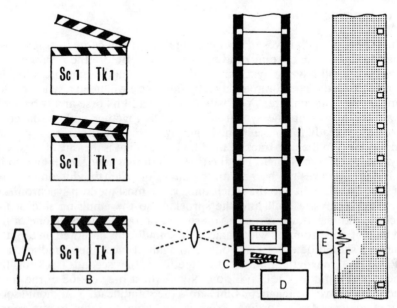

Synchronizing sound and picture. The clapper board, fully closed at B, recorded on film at C, sends signal via microphone A and amplifier D to head E, registering signal on magnetic film F.

the synchronizer, check again to make sure they are still level, then wind on. You can carry on winding until the end of the take. Then either sound will go dead or you will run out of picture. You will lose synchronization at that point, as filming was discontinued. Mark a level cutting point on both sound and picture and remove the picture from the synchronizer. Wind on the sound by hand until you hear the sound identification of the next scene and take number. Find the appropriate scene on the action and again mark up the clap on the soundtrack and the corresponding point in the action. Replace the action in the synchronizer, making sure that the two wax pencil marks identifying the start of this second scene and take are level. Now you can wind back until you come to the wax pencil cutting point you have already marked on the magnetic track. Put a mark on the action of the new shot at this point. Now you can join the first shot to the second. If you join on the two points you have marked, you will be sure to have both scenes in synchronization. You can then carry on in this manner to the end of the reel. When you rewind the reels you can add the slate numbers to the identification written on the leaders: DEATH IN VENICE Slates 26–35 ACTION on the picture, and DEATH IN VENICE slates 26–35 MAG on the sound. If the reels get put back in the wrong cans after projection you will find the correct reels are easier to identify if they are clearly marked.

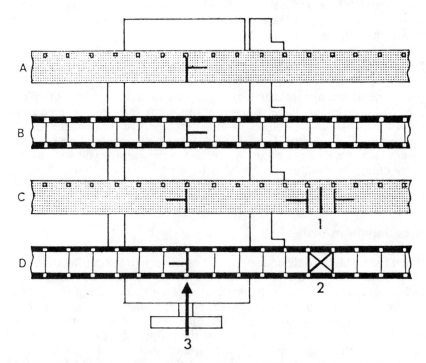

Synchronizing rushes: the cut from first to second sync shot. (C) Outgoing magnetic sound. (D) Outgoing picture. (A) Incoming magnetic. (B) Incoming picture. (1 and 2) Sync marks. (3) Synchronizer hand-turning wheel.

Points it pays to check

There are several points to remember when synchronizing rushes. First of all, never cut off the identification. You should not attempt to make an artistic job of it. Synchronizing rushes is like sandpapering woodwork before painting–a necessary but dull part of the preparation. Always check your camera and sound information sheets carefully before you start work. Sometimes you will find the clapper board is on the end of a take and you have to synchronize the scene from the end and work backwards. A few minutes spent looking at the information sheets can save hours of searching for clapper boards at points where they have never been photographed. Do not expect to find every scene that has been shot. By no means all photographed scenes are printed by the laboratory. If a scene is no good the cameraman will mark on his sheets a large N.G. At the end of the day's filming, the cameraman will go through his sheets and mark the takes which the laboratory is to print. Only these takes will reach you in positive form, although everything filmed will be on the processed master material. The same situation applies with sound. If the film has been photographed in a studio, the sound may have been recorded straight on magnetic film. If, however, much of the work has been done on location, sound will probably have been recorded on quarter-inch tape and transferred to magnetic film after filming has been completed in the way I have already described. Here again, not all takes will have been transferred. You can save yourself the search for scenes and takes which have not been printed or re-recorded by looking at the information sheets before you start to synchronize the rushes.

Viewing rushes

When sound and picture match exactly, you can take the reels of film to a preview theatre. In a large studio every morning the director, editor and other leading technicians and sometimes members of the cast sit and view the rushes. The director decides which takes he wishes to use and which scenes he wants to shoot again. At the end of the viewing you will possibly be given a rough outline of the takes he would like you to use. You can then return to the cutting room and start making your first rough assembly (the *rough cut*).

Breaking down rushes

When the rushes have been viewed you can return to the cutting room and start *breaking down* the rushes. Wind through and separate each scene, and possibly each take. On the start of the shot write, with a wax pencil, the scene and take number, and then hang the length of film in the trim bin. If it is a very long shot it may be coiled up and held together with an elastic band. Check each scene against the script, or if there is no script, make a detailed shot list. Mark the type of shot, whether long-shot or close-up, the subject and the action and then hang the shot in the bin. Write the number on the film itself and on the trim bin above the clip on which it hangs.

As you break down each scene, make sure that the laboratory has printed through the key numbers on the edge of the film. Those numbers will be vital when you come to match the edited cutting print to your master material. If you find they are missing before you start to cut, send the reel of print back with the appropriate reel of negative to the laboratory. They will then number the two in ink and return them to you as soon as possible. Anyone who has had the misfortune to edit a film which has not been edge numbered, and not noticed the error until the cutting has been done, will agree that this simple check of the rushes before cutting begins is well worth while. If the numbers are not there when you come to neg cut you will have to eye-match every shot and every cutting point, and with a picture 16 mm in size that is a nightmare even for one cut. Having to eye-match an entire film is a prospect which does not even bear thinking about.

Checking the master

When the master negative is processed the lab may retain the uncut master until it is ready to be neg cut or return it to you with the rush print. If they return it you will be presented with several cans of mute print and a corresponding amount of negative or reversal master. Before you do anything else, check the negative to make sure that it is all there. It may be several weeks before you actually need to use the negative again. By that time your print will be in an entirely different form and you will be unable to remember if there were originally ten or twenty rolls. Looking for material mislaid several weeks before is always a complicated and unsatisfying task. When you are satisfied that the right number of reels of negative and print have been delivered, it is quite a good idea to wind through the negative on a flat rewinder. This should be done with immense care. Always wear white linen gloves when you are working with negative, for any mark you put on the negative will remain there and blemish all prints made from the material thereafter. Master materials must never be projected. They can, however, be wound from one reel to another on the flat rewind. Hold your left hand on the extreme edges of the film and you will feel the point where the reels of negative removed from the camera have been spliced together by the processing laboratory. The laboratory, when processing the exposed materials, develop each reel and then splice the various short reels together to make a more acceptable length with which to load the printing machines. Normally a laboratory will join up a number of 100 ft rolls, and probably join two or three 400 ft rolls into one. They will not in any sense cut the rolls. Blank spacing and fogged scenes will all be left on. When they have an acceptable length roll they will load the film on the printer and produce your cutting print.

Logging rushes

Before you start to cut by breaking down the reels of rushes into individual shots, all the scenes and takes should be *logged*. Put the cutting copy in a synchronizer and arm yourself with a pen and paper. The purpose of logging is to enable you to immediately identify the origin of every foot of film and every scene and take when the rushes have been cut. So, put the film in the synchronizer and wind down to the first slate. Make a note of the scene and slate number and alongside on your sheets note the nearest edge number and the camera roll number. Wind down to the start of the next take and repeat the process. You have now given yourself a detailed cross-reference which will help you to identify any part of that first scene and take. In your fine cut you may only use a couple of feet of that scene and take, and you certainly won't use the slate, but if your print gets damaged or if you want to extend a shot or order an optical effect, edge numbers on the film and the log sheets you have prepared will make the job simple.

Ink edge numbers

Ink numbers are sometimes used in addition to the latent image numbers normally found on picture stock. Some editors like to have cutting-copy sound and picture ink numbered after the rushes have been synchronized and before cutting starts. It simply provides an immediate visual synchronization check and makes it much easier to find trims. When you have synchronized the rushes you can send your cutting-copy action and sound off to be ink numbered (or *rubber numbered*, as it's often called). A laboratory will be able to do the work for you. They will print ink numbers at regular intervals (usually every 20 frames) on the cutting-copy action and then print the same numbers starting at the same point on the cutting-copy sound. As you have already synchronized sound and picture you only have to match the ink numbers to get an immediate sync check. If you are working with a video picture a time-code can be printed on the mag in a similar way.

The first assembly

The main purpose of a first rough assembly is to put the shots which have been photographed in the order dictated by the script. At this stage no attempt should be made to cut the shots to length or to edit them for effect. The object is to see first of all if they will go together in the right order, smoothly and without jarring the action.

When the rushes have been synchronized and numbered, you can get down to making your first rough assembly. First look at the script and at any notes made when the rushes were viewed. If there seems to be only one take of the first shot, look for it in the trim bin. If you are making a mute first assembly, or rough cut as it is more often called, you can work on practically any kind of machine. A picture synchronizer is ideal, as is almost any kind of power-operated editing machine. If you are really short of equipment and the film has been shot mute, this first stage of the work can be done with an animated viewer and a pair of rewind arms. With shot one in your hand, you can place it in whatever machine you are using. Run down to the start of the shot, losing the spacing and any fogged part of the picture and cutting off the clapper board. If there is action, mark the point where you want to cut in. Suppose the scene shows three men in an office talking. Wind through and look at the first part of the action. At the start of the shot they appear to be frozen. Although there is no sound you can almost hear the director calling for silence and then action. Then they all begin to move. One man picks up a telephone. Another passes the third man a cup of coffee. A secretary appears from out of shot and hands the man at the desk a pile of papers, then she disappears. Where should you cut in?

The script lists this as an office interior over which commentary will eventually be heard. For sound it lists only general office hubbub and gives details of the commentator's words. Have another look at the start of the shot. Wind through it carefully until you have found the exact frame where the action starts. Mark it with your wax pencil and join a leader or a piece of white spacing to it. Allow enough spacing to thread up a projector–about 15 ft will probably suffice–and mark on the front of it the title of the film and the fact that this is the cutting copy. A plain 'C/C' is all that is needed. Then mark 'Reel I ACTION'. You will then have no difficulty in identifying it. What is far more important, it will not be lost if an absentminded projectionist puts it in the wrong can and sends it to someone else after a viewing. Always identify everything.

With a leader on the start of the film, you will be able to take up the film on a spool and return to consider the shot which forms the start of the action. You now have to find a place to cut out of the shot. Until commentary has been recorded and laid, you cannot be quite certain where it should be, for obviously you will try to match the action to the requirements of the dialogue as accurately as possible. At this stage, when the work of editing is just beginning, it pays to leave everything rather longer than you really want. It is always easier to trim a shot later, when commentary has been recorded, than to find and replace the piece of film you have removed. You may decide later that you want it back again. Sometimes, you are bound to find that a shot needs to be even longer than you anticipated. The parts of a shot which you do not use should always be replaced in the trim bin after a cut has been made. This does not, of course, apply to material which is obviously useless. Fogged shots and other misfortunates can be committed to the waste bin. Extra lengths of usable material should be returned to the trim bin in case at a later stage you decide you want to extend the shot or alter your cutting point. Everyone has his own particular system for filing trims. I personally like to write the shot number or some brief identification – 'Ext hotel', 'CU Jack', and so on. If the shots have been ink numbered the numbers will be probably be enough identification.

Where to cut?

Let us return to the scene in the office. At the start there is a sudden burst of activity, then the girl enters and leaves her pile of papers with the man at the desk. She leaves and the hubbub continues for a few frames before the action is stopped. Now where should you cut out? If you cut when the secretary hands over the papers, you may well be wrong. If the director had wanted to cut there, why would he have kept the action going until the girl walked out of shot? Check the script again and see if there is any detailed cutting point listed. Does it say:

```
1 INT. OFFICE DAY. M.S. SECRETARY ENTERS AND PASSES PAPERS
               TO DIRECTOR


2 INT. OFFICE DAY. C.U. DIRECTOR TAKES PAPERS AND LOOKS AT THEM
```

Or is the next scene entirely different, filmed perhaps at a different location? If so, and this is an isolated office scene which is not part of a sequence photographed at the same location, you will have more freedom to choose your cutting point. In the example in question, it might look neater to wait until the secretary walks out of shot, rather than cut in the middle of her movement. There are very few hard and fast rules but you will soon see if a cut works or looks unnatural. In an action sequence cuts in the middle of movement can be very effective. If you cut where the secretary is half way across the room between the desk and the edge of the shot, you will not be committing a cardinal error, but it may look better if you wait until she goes out of shot.

There can be no cast-iron rules about where you should cut. With experience, you will find you can sense the right point. The only way to get that feeling of whether a cut works or not is to try making a first assembly and then sit down and view it. You will find you learn a lot, and you will then look at films which other people have cut with new eyes.

Perhaps the second sequence you have to assemble shows a lorry on a demolition site. A bulldozer is shunting to and fro moving large amounts of rubble, which it shovels into the lorry. Where should you cut into and out of this kind of shot? Look at it carefully and note the exact movements of the bulldozer. It digs into the rubble and then lifts it up and reverses. It stops, turns and moves towards the lorry. It then tips the rubble into the back of the lorry, reverses and moves back for another load. Now, where should you cut? There are plenty of possibilities. The bulldozer lunges into the rubble and shovels it up, then raises its mechanical grab. There is a slight pause when the grab has been hoisted whilst the driver changes gear. He reverses. There is another pause whilst he again changes gear before advancing to the lorry. When the load has been tipped there is another pause—and so on. Cut in any of these pauses and it will probably look all right, but match the action carefully. Before you cut check the script and find out what part of the operation the film is supposed to be showing. If the commentary is talking about the versatile mechanical grab which can dig into anything with ease you may decide to cut to the close-up earlier. If it is talking about the bulldozer's ability to move over rough ground you may want to spend more time on the long-shot. Assembly editing is largely a matter of commonsense – a question of *matching the action* when cutting from shot to shot.

Matching action cuts

If you have to cut together two shots of someone walking, you will soon appreciate the importance of matching the action when you cut and of being frame-accurate when you do so. First, make sure that the two shots you have to cut together have been photographed from acceptably different angles. It is quite acceptable to cut from a long-shot to a mid-shot or from a mid-shot to a close-up, or indeed from a front view to a profile. It is not, however, acceptable to cut from one shot of a man walking to another shot of the same man walking if the two shots have been taken from a similar distance and at the same angle. If that has happened you will need to insert a *cutaway*.

Let us first assume that you have to cut together two shots showing a man walking down a street. One is a long-shot, the other a mid-shot. Where should you cut? The answer, as is the case with so much assembly-editing technique, is really a matter of common sense. Look at the action and mark the point where his feet are in one particular position. Perhaps his left foot is flat on the ground, and his right foot is just leaving it. His right toe is bent and his heel is about the same level as the ankle of his left foot. That is on the long-shot. Now look at the incoming mid-shot and select an identical position.Cut the two together and check them to make sure that the action is smooth, and make any adjustment necessary. If you do not match the action carefully the picture will seem to jump and the scene will look unnatural.

If later in the sequence the man stops and lights a cigarette and you have to cut from mid-shot to close-up, make the cut before he takes out his lighter and cigarettes or when he is actually lighting them, with his hand comparatively still, and not when his arm is in mid-air between pocket and face. Always match the action when you cut from shot to shot.

Cutting on movement

You will note that I have suggested cutting when movement is minimized. That advice holds good for many situations but there are also times when it is better to cut as the action takes place. Cutting as someone turns, as a blow is aimed or in similar situations can work very well providing you avoid a double take by matching the action at the point at which you cut. Experiment for yourself and after a while you will instinctively feel when a cut does or does not work. When it does not work you will find it is disturbing to watch. When it does work a cut can pass almost unnoticed. Some editors feel it is best to cut just before or just after a movement. Others feel that by cutting mid-action the cut can be disguised; and if it is made at precisely the right point, that is true. The important thing is to avoid cutting at any point which jars and looks unnatural.

Using cutaways

There will be occasions when you will not be able to match the action of two comparable shots. Perhaps the scenes have been badly directed or photographed by someone who does not know much about editing. Let us look again at the example of the man walking along a street. Let us assume this time that the script calls for two shots, one showing him entering one end of the street and another showing him leaving the opposite end. No good editor will be able to cut the two scenes together, unless the scenes have been very carefully photographed in a manner which disguises the fact that the man is in fact walking a very long walk in the space of a few seconds. If a shot of one end of the street with a man in it is cut straight on to another shot of the other end of a street with the same man in it, the action will appear extremely unnatural. So, how can you cope with this sort of situation?

You can solve the problem by using a cutaway. A cutaway is basically either a cover-up for poor continuity or an indication of the passing of time. The nature of, and the need for, cutaways is best described by giving an example. Imagine you are cutting an interview with someone arriving at an airport. The camera has been set up facing the person being interviewed. He arrives and the camera records his answers to the questions put to him. The camera remains on him, and him alone. The director, standing beside the camera, listens to the answers and realizes that he will not want to use part of the answer given to one of the questions. He wants to use the beginning and the end of the man's answer but not the middle of it.

The director knows that, as the camera has not been moved since the start of the interview, to omit the offending sentence will be impossible without jarring the action. If he asks you to simply cut out the words he doesn't like, the man being interviewed will appear to jump where the piece of film has been removed. The director knows that sound is being recorded on separate tape and you will be editing sound and picture on two separate pieces of film so, when the interview is over, he moves the camera round to concentrate on the man who is asking the questions. The man being interviewed does not feature in the shot. The camera is run, without running the sound equipment, and a silent shot of the interviewer listening is obtained. When you edit this sequence you will be able to cut the dialogue at the point where the man's comments are not wanted. At the same point you can cut out of the shot of the man being questioned and into the shot of the interviewer. The remainer of the required dialogue can be overlaid over the shot of the interviewer. At a suitable point you can cut back to show the shot of the man who is speaking. The intermediate shot of the interviewer is known as a cutaway.

Variety of cutaways

Cutaways can take many forms. Take the case of that man walking down the length of a street, for example. It would be quite acceptable to cut from a shot of the man entering one end of the street to a shot of someone watching him from a nearby window, and back to him walking towards the opposite end of the street. An alternative would be to cut from the first shot to a close-up of his feet walking on the pavement, then back to the street shot. The movements of the feet must be matched on the cut and only the feet and pavement must appear in the close-up, without showing the surroundings. The intermediate cutaway shots I have suggested distract the audience slightly from the main course of the action and allow an otherwise unacceptable cut to be made without trouble.

Cutaways must, of course, always be relevant. You cannot just put in any old shot you happen to have spare. Choose one which refers to the action in question, and cut it carefully. In the case of the spectator watching the man walking down the street, make sure he or she is looking in the right direction. If in the first shot the man is right of screen, the person in the cutaway must be looking from left to right. Do everything you can to ensure that one shot follows another as smoothly as possible so you do not arouse the audience's suspicions.

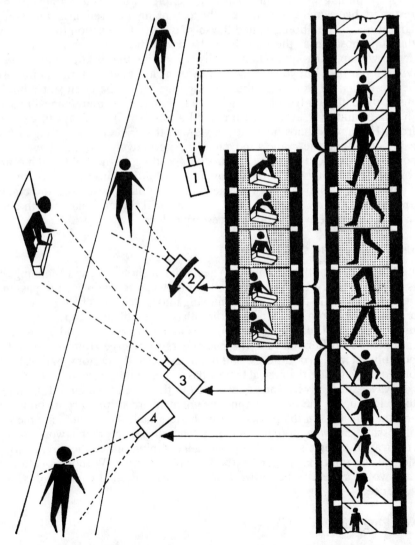

Using cutaways. Scene 1: man enters one end of street. Scene 4: man leaves opposite end of street. Scenes 2 and 3 are possible cutaways.

Using cutaways to solve problems

Let us consider some further examples. Consider a sequence showing equipment being loaded on to a ship. The purpose of the sequence is to show how a new car is loaded into a ship's hold. The car is first driven on to a wooden platform, which is then hoisted up by crane and swung out over the open hold of the ship. In the normal course of events, the car and platform would be lowered straight down to the hold but, when the cameraman was filming this scene, the crane driver had some technical trouble and there was quite a long pause between the car reaching the top of the hold and being lowered down into it. The cameraman therefore stopped filming. When he heard the crane motor starting again, he restarted his camera and filmed the car being lowered into the hold. Unfortunately he photographed the second part of the action from exactly the same position as the first. Now if you cut the two shots together the action will appear to jump unnaturally. A cut like that is known as a *jump cut*. It looks bad, but you can avoid it by using a cutaway. Mark a point just before the crane stops with the car suspended over the open ship's hold. Insert the cutaway. If he knows what he is doing, the cameraman will have shot one, and may even have provided a number of cutaways to choose from. He may perhaps have shot a view of the crane driver sitting in his cab, controlling the crane's movement. Alternatively, he may have shot down into the hold showing the dockers waiting in the hold looking up towards the camera. There are many possibilities. Insert one of these cutaways, and then cut back to the shot at a point just before the crane lowers the car into the hold. The action should then appear smooth and natural and there will be no unnecessary delays.

Using cutaways to shorten time

Let's consider another example. When you cut shots of aircraft landing, it is often necessary to condense the time between touchdown, the passengers alighting, and the passengers moving into the customs hall. Here again a straight cut from one scene to the other may not be acceptable. Time must be allowed for the aircraft to pass along the runway and across the tarmac and further time for the passengers to emerge from the aircraft, possibly get into airport buses, and finally arrive in the customs hall. A shot of people watching the arrival from a passenger building could be used as a cutaway. Alternatively you could cut from the shot of the aircraft landing to a close-up of the arrivals announcement board in the airport building and then to shots of the passengers in the terminal. Again there are plenty of possible cutaways. What would not generally be acceptable would be to cut straight from a shot of the passengers coming out of the aircraft to a shot of the same passengers in the terminal building. Without a cutaway they would appear to be in two places at once, and that could confuse an audience.

Working without cutaways

Sometimes you will find the cameraman has not filmed any cutaways. When that happens you may have a problem. You will have a glaring continuity error and no obvious cure for it. What can you do about it? There are two alternative solutions. Take the aircraft arrival scene, for example. If the cameraman has had the good sense to let the aeroplane pass out of shot in the first exposure (the actual landing) he may also have been wise enough to start his camera before the plane comes into shot in front of the customs hall. In a case like this you could, as a last resort, cut from one to the other, making sure that the plane was actually out of shot when the cut was made. Sound, skilfully laid and mixed at later date, would do something to smooth out the rather poor continuity. A far better remedy would be to dissolve or 'mix' from one shot to the other. This kind of effect is known as an *optical*; we shall be looking at the ways in which opticals are used later.

Missing scenes

As you continue with your first rough assembly you may sometimes find that shots listed in the script are missing. Perhaps they have not yet been shot, or maybe the director has planned to use a library stock shot at this particular point. Later on you will have to find this material and cut it in. For the first rough cut, however, you can simply build the shot up with spacing, marking on it the appropriate scene number and the words 'scene missing'.

More about matching action cuts

You will often find you have to cut together sequences of shots featuring the same characters all shot at the same location. When you are cutting together more than one view of the same subject you must take very great care to match the outgoing and incoming actions precisely. Consider, for example, a sequence showing three people eating in a restaurant. The script explains what the shots are all about:

SCENE 1   Int. Restaurant Day. LS. Three people sit at table eating.
          We see there is one man and his wife and young son. The son
          is looking eagerly at a waiter who approaches the table with
          an ice-cream.

SCENE 2   Int. Restaurant Day. CMS. The waiter hands the boy the
          ice-cream. The boy takes it and drops it on the table cloth.

SCENE 3   Int. Restaurant Day. CU. The boy tries to scoop up the ice-
          cream with his spoon, hoping his father has not noticed
          that he has spilled it.

When you cut those three simple shots together you have every opportunity to make a series of continuity errors. When cutting shots one and two together you must take care to match the action exactly. Note where the ice-cream is in relation to both the waiter and the boy at the end of the first shot, and find the corresponding position in the incoming exposure. Now look for a place where the action is the same and where there is a minimum of movement. Are they holding the ice-cream with their hands in the same position? Is the boy looking down or up? Are all the points at the end of the first shot the same as those at the beginning of the second one? If you are sure they are not different, cut the scenes together and run through until you find a suitable point to cut to the third exposure.

A cut tends to make the action in a sequence more noticeable. As the boy drops the ice-cream, a cut would tend to slightly emphasize his nervousness. It may be possible to hold the second shot until he has actually dropped the ice-cream and looked up to see if his father has noticed. This would be quite a good thing to do. Then cut to the close-up. By cutting at that point you are emphasizing the boy's reaction and reminding the audience that he is worried in case anyone else has noticed. Match the angle of his hand, the position of the ice-cream and all the other small items. Make sure that if he has his mouth open at the end of the outgoing shot it is open at the point you cut to the new one. When you are sure that the action is the same, make your cut. The three shots will then seem to go together naturally.

The same principle holds good for almost every situation. You must match the action at the start and end of each shot forming part of a sequence. If you are cutting shots filmed in a factory showing someone working at a lathe and the man is seen working on the same lathe in consecutive shots, the action must be matched exactly, or a cutaway must be inserted. Cut from long-shot to close-up, from mid-shot to close-up or any alternative shot where the perspective is different. If the man has one hand on the controls in the mid-shot make sure it is still there in the close-up. If he is looking ahead of him in the first shot, do not let him look down when you cut to the second view or his head will appear to jump.

Cutting action is not really complicated. It is simply a matter of common sense and observation. With a little care and practice you will find your first rough cut will run quite smoothly. At the end of the first rough cut you should have everything in the right running order. Some of the scenes will probably be over-length, but the basic materials for further work will be there. Some shots may be missing. Perhaps they are to be photographed later, or maybe no plans have been made for the cameraman to shoot them at all. If that is the case you may have use stock shots of *library material*.

Using library material

Most stock-shot film libraries hold quite a wide range of general materials. Long-shots and more detailed views of large cities and country scenes, and shots of well-known people and places, are usually available. You will find different libraries tend to specialize in different types of material. The television networks, for example, are an excellent source of news footage; shots from television documentary programmes can often be purchased for use as stock shots. Other libraries may have fine collections of natural history shots or sporting events. You may need to look around. You will be astonished at the variety of shots you can find. I needed some shots of someone eating fire for a TV documentary and I got them from a library. If you look around, unless the subject you need is very specialist, like a particular type of car in a specific street, you will often find it. Most major film production companies have a library of some kind. A number of specialist organizations also exist solely to supply still and cine library materials. Some of these libraries have another function. If you cannot go abroad to film general background shots for a particular production, the library will possibly be able to get the material for you. They may themselves have the shots you want. Alternatively they may have contacts who can produce the required material from the country concerned.

Fees and royalties

Before you use any library material, find out how much it is going to cost and, above all, make sure the copyright is owned by the person who is selling it to you.

The next step is for you to go to see what material they can offer. Normally a small search fee is charged for finding the material, and a viewing machine or cinema is provided where prints of the shots they have selected can be viewed. If they have the kind of scene you are looking for, you will be able to order a copy of the shot in question. You will be charged all laboratory costs and a royalty fee. This is usually at a fixed amount per foot of film. When the film is finally edited, measure the amount of each shot you use and let the library know how much you have used. The sum you have to pay will depend on the amount of material you have used and the type of audience the finished film is to be shown to. Shots used in a film intended for showing to a factory's own employees will cost less than the same shots used in a film for cinema or television showing. If the film is to be released all over the world the cost will be higher than if it is only going to be used in one country. Films for advertising are the most expensive of all.

Libraries may sometimes seem very expensive, but if you work out the cost of shooting some of the scenes they provide you may find that the charges are not that unreasonable. A simple shot like a general view of an airport can be quite expensive to film when you have first of all to pay for permission to film there, and then meet the cost of film stock, processing and the camera crew and equipment needed to photograph it. A library shot can save time and money, but don't overdo it. Always try to find library shots which are not already familiar and when you are looking for stock shots make sure you provide the library with an adequate brief.

Ordering library material

If you need anything from a library the first step to take is to write and tell the library exactly what you want. Let them know the name and nature of your production and give them the basic details of the shot you require. Tell them the date of the material you are looking for. It is absolutely useless asking for stock shots of Times Square and then trying to cut the scenes any librarian would normally provide to meet a present-day request into a film dealing with New York in the early 1930s. However, if you want material on Times Square in 1930, say so, and you may well find the libraries have got it. That may sound stupid advice, but a number of film-makers tend to complain that they cannot get material when the real problem is that they simply have not given enough details of what they are looking for.

Working with dupes

Stock-shot libraries will not, of course, part with their original material. They will supply you with a *dupe* (duplicate) and a cutting print to work with. A lot of library film was originally shot on 35 mm. Some 16 mm library shots are negative and some are on reversal. Whatever the format of the original, you can still get a suitable 16 mm dupe for your production if you tell the library exactly what you want. Tell them what your original footage is, so it and the library dupe can be intercut. If your film is shot on 16 mm colour negative a 16 mm reversal dupe master of the library shot isn't going to be much good. You want an *inter-negative*, which is the same way round as the emulsion of your original. If the library shot is only available on 35 mm colour negative and you are working with 16 mm original colour negative film, a 16 mm *reduction CRI* is what you want. Tell the laboratory what the film you are cutting was shot on. They will then supply a dupe you can intercut. If the library material is only available on video you can arrange for the tape to be recorded on film but do not expect the quality to look the same as a film original. The line structure of the TV signal will always show and the definition will not be particularly good, but when no other material is available it may suffice. Always ask for a cutting print from the dupe. Make sure there are edge numbers which are clear. If they are missing or unreadable have the dupe and cutting copy ink numbered before you start to cut.

At what stage of editing should you order library material? There is no set rule to obey, although there is usually an ultimate deadline to meet. When your edited print is matched to the original material the negative or duplicate colour master of your library material will be needed in the course of completing the work. If you want to see the results on a screen you will have to order a print from your duplicate materials and the print can then be edited into the cutting copy. You can thus order your library material at any time provided it is ready in time to cut into the final edited version negative or colour master. It is wise to leave a margin of time in case any unexpected problems arise in the course of making the duplicate materials.

Damaged stock shots

You may sometimes find you have to work with stock shots which are in a poor state of repair. Fortunately most libraries are very good at looking after materials entrusted to their care. Sometimes, however, you may need to use a shot provided by some person or organization not really professionally film-minded. It is quite possible that the shot they provide will be either scratched or dirty. As much damage as possible must be repaired before the shot is incorporated in your finished production. Ask the laboratory to clean the master material. It is absolutely useless trying to do anything with a duplicate in which all the faults of the original have been copied, but if you have access to the original you may be able to improve the situation. With immense care you clean it with a dry anti-static cloth, or one which has been moistened with carbon tetrachloride. If you hold the film at an angle to the light you will then be able to see any scratches. If the scratches are on the emulsion side, there is little you can do to remedy them. At best you can clean them up a bit and possibly make them rather less noticeable. If, however, they are on the cellulose side of the film, they can very possibly be removed. There are a number of chemical processes which can give good results. Many laboratories will also be able to polish the offending scratch until it is not noticeable. All this is well worth doing if you want to obtain the best possible quality from library material.

Using archive film

If you ever need to use really old film materials you are faced with an additional problem. Film shot years ago was photographed at an entirely different speed. Many early cameras were, of course, hand cranked, and the movement and exposure on many old shots is a long way from the standards nowadays required. Old film shown on present-day machines at sound speed tends to look jerky and unevenly exposed, but there is a way of remedying this fault. It is known as *stretch printing*.

Stretch printing

When a film is stretch-printed, every second frame is printed twice. That helps to smooth out the jerkiness of action, and in cases of extreme difference, the printer light can be adjusted to compensate for irregular exposure. If you have to use old film in a production you are cutting you will probably want to have it stretch-printed. If you are using library material, you will not be able to have the original but will have to make do with a duplicate. Make sure this is stretch-printed. If you are, however, lucky enough to obtain the original material you will still have to use a duplicate in your final edited version. If you intercut an ordinary dupe of the old material with the new material specially photographed for the production, the laboratory will print both as they stand for projection at present-day sound speeds. They cannot stretch-print part of a reel. You must first have the material you want stretch-printed, and then cut the stretch-printed duplicate into the edited material. The laboratory can produce further prints for you from this.

If you are using library material, and you are supplied with an old-speed fine-grain film, ask the laboratory to stretch-print a duplicate negative for you. They can make a print for editing from this, and you will be able to cut the negative into the edited final version of your picture. You will find a detailed explanation of how to obtain dupes from the various film formats in the last chapter.

Disadvantages of library material

There are two main kinds of occasion when stock shots are useful. The first of these occasions is when the material needed cannot be obtained in any other way, as is the case with news film and much historical material. The second occasion is when the cost of photographing the required shot is not justified, for it would cost more to send a camera team out to shoot the shot again than it would to include library footage. The first reason is a good one but, in my opinion, the second reason is too often used as an excuse.

Many original views of well-known landmarks can still be obtained, yet too often producers insist on using the same old library exposures. Think, for example, of the number of times Big Ben, the London Houses of Parliament and the Statue of Liberty have been included in films. On too many of these occasions the same shots have been used. No doubt they serve their purpose. They identify the locations, and when a film cannot justify the cost of sending a cameraman out on location the library shots will suffice, but if the cost can be met it is surely worth trying to get something more original.

Library material can prove quite expensive. Remember you have two bills to pay. You have to meet all the laboratory costs involved in making the duplicate materials for you to cut, and you also have to pay a royalty based on the amount of film used in your final edited version. The main drawback is usually quality. A lot of library film is very old, and it shows. The quality of dupes is never as good as of original material. Recent improvements in film stock have done much to improve the film quality of library shots. The CRI process alone, by cutting out the intermediate positive stage, can get amazing results, but for optimum quality it is still best to use a minimum of library material.

5

Fine editing technique

The editing of sound and picture go very closely together, especially when you are trying to achieve a particular mood or atmosphere in a film or a sequence. The overall pace of a film is governed by the action in the story, which in turn suggests how it should be cut. Generally speaking, slow cutting from scene to scene tends to create a rather more relaxed atmosphere than cutting together a series of short scenes quickly one after the other. Sound, and changes of sound, tend to emphasize a change in mood. By cutting slowly from scene to scene to start with, and gradually increasing the pace by making each shot slightly shorter than the one which precedes it, tension can be gradually increased.

Consider, for example, scenes of a police car chasing a motorcycle through the streets of a big city. At the start of the chase you may have a long-shot of the motorbike roaring away, followed by the police car. Perhaps the shot is held for five seconds. A second shot, showing only the motorbike, could again be held for five seconds, as could a third shot showing only the car. Cut then to the motorbike, holding the shot for five seconds. The motor-cyclist looks over his shoulder at the police car and as he turns you cut to a shot of the car. You hold that for only three seconds before cutting back to the bike. Tension is increasing. Give three seconds more on the motorbike, then a shot of the man riding it, held only for two seconds. A shot of the bike approaching traffic lights, held for three seconds. The lights changing to red is the subject of a two-second close-up. The bike skids and crashes, shown in two seconds. In two more seconds the police car skids to a halt. We cut to a longer shot as the policemen get out. This shot is held for four seconds. A longer shot still shows them walk over to the motor-cyclist trapped under his machine. This shot is held for five seconds, and we are back where we started. The tension is over. It started where the chase started and ended when the motor-cycle skidded. As it grew more tense the scenes followed each other more quickly and the drama of the situation was thus increased.

Shot length and pace

The length of time you hold each shot can be used to emphasize a particular point or situation. In a conversation, to give one of many examples, if you are intercutting shots of two people involved in the conversation and want to emphasize one person more than the other, you can do so by holding his shot for rather longer than a shot of the other person. Imagine a simple argument, told in five shots. The action each time shows the person who is speaking. The dialogue goes like this:

```
SHOT 1  MAN 1:  I suppose you think you are clever?
SHOT 2  MAN 2:  Not particularly.
SHOT 3  MAN 1:  Then why did you do it?
SHOT 4  MAN 2:  Because I thought it was necessary.
SHOT 5  MAN 1:  What a silly thing to do.
```

Those shots can be cut together in several different ways. You could keep each shot long, cutting to it a second or so before the dialogue is spoken, and holding it to observe the speaker's immediate reactions. If you do that you will make the situation relatively undramatic, especially if all your shots are of the same length. By making the second and fourth shots shorter than the first, third and fifth you will immediately increase the tension. You will make the first man more aggressive, and the exchange will immediately become more interesting. Alternatively you can make the first and second shots of equal length, and hold the third shot for half as long again. 'Then why did you do it?' The shot is held for just long enough to stimulate that tiny bit of curiosity and extra interest. If you then cut quickly from the fourth shot to the fifth you will make the first man's summary more emphatic. By altering these cuts in the different ways I have suggested you can slightly emphasize different sides of an argument.

Action cuts

With action cutting, where you are not concerned with dialogue, there is much more scope for really creative editing. Let us consider the building up of tension in another action sequence. The sequence this time deals with the journey of a munitions train through occupied France in the last war. The train contains two carriages of soldiers and much equipment. It is going fast through the night and the driver is unaware that a few miles up the line Resistance workers are mining the track ready to blow up the train when it passes. In the script, the action is intercut between scenes of soliders getting drunk on the train, the driver coaxing the train to make greater speed, the wheels of the train turning, and Resistance workers wiring fuses several miles up the line. The script simply points out that the scenes have to be cut together. Editing has to make the scene dramatic, for no dialogue is spoken.

Dramatic situations

It would, of course, be perfectly possible to make all the scenes the same length, but the situation would lack a great deal of drama. It is far better to try to make the scenes more tense by varying the length of the shots as the train nears disaster. Try first of all to understand the dramatic situation. In the train there are two groups of people – soldiers who are not worried about time, and a train driver and his colleague who are. Farther up the line are the Resistance workers, also worried about being caught and very anxious to get the job over before the train comes in sight. With this situation in mind you can form a basic plan of operation.

You may decide to make your shots of the soldiers longer than the remainder. Start with a general outline of the overall position and shots of each of the three main situations, held for round about ten seconds. It might be a good idea to start with the driver and then cut from the soldiers to the Resistance, and then cut back to the train driver again. From the comparatively silent situation two miles up the line, the cut to the noise of the engine will itself have considerable impact. Hold this shot for a shorter period, then go back up the line. This shot again should be shorter than on the previous occasion. Then go back to the soldiers, holding the shot for a few seconds longer. Cut to the train driver, holding the shot for just a few seconds, then cut back to the Resistance. We can hear the train in the distance now. Hold this shot for longer than you held the shot of the driver – possibly about twice the length – and then cut back to the train. Hold it for a few seconds less than the shot you are cutting away from and then cut back again. Hold the shot of the Resistance waiting, having planted their charges, for a couple of seconds longer than you held the train racing towards them. Cut back to a close-up of the train wheels. If you held the Resistance shot for five seconds hold the wheels for just three. Show the driver for 2 seconds and then the explosion. The following shots can be held for as long as necessary, for the tension will be over. The exact time you hold each shot is up to you, but by varying your cutting pace you can do much to bring the scene to life.

There are, of course, many ways in which you can assemble a scene of this nature. I have suggested one of them. Others may be much better but the one I have given will at least give you an idea of how altering the length of each shot can lend drama to, and shift emphasis from, any situation. I hope to encourage you to make your own experiments. That is the best way to learn editing. The examples I have given have been of dramatic situations but the principles they illustrate apply equally well to film shot by any film unit anywhere. Leave all your shots the same length, and the audience will fall asleep before the film finishes. Vary the tempo and you will keep them interested from beginning to end. Even a machine has its own kind of tempo. Study its movements, and work out your shots and cuts accordingly. You will find the time is well spent: the discoveries you make will not be disappointing.

Gradual transitions

In the examples I have just given we changed from scene to scene by means of a cut. There are several ways of moving from one shot or sequence to another. If you do not want to cut directly from one shot to the next you can gradually merge the two scenes until one replaces the other. The first shot dissolves to the second and for a moment the action becomes a mixture of both shots before becoming only the second shot. This method of transition is called simoly *dissolving*, or more often, in television, *mixing*, from one scene to another. Alternatively you can *fade out* the first shot and *fade in* the second, with a brief period of blackness in between the two exposures. These effects, which can take many forms, are known as *optical effects*.

Using opticals

Traditionally, dissolves were used to denote the passing of time. If shot two was supposed to take place some time after shot one, the editor would arrange to dissolve from one scene to the other. Nowadays this doctrine is often disregarded and a straight cut is sometimes made, care being taken to ensure that the scene is different enough to avoid the jarring effect caused by cutting two similar scenes together.

Sometimes editors use a dissolve because they simply cannot cut two shots together without a jump in the action. Perhaps the scene has been badly directed or photographed, and there is a pause in the action after which, without a change of scene, the action is started again. To cut the two pieces of action together by simply removing the part of the scene where nothing is happening would make an unacceptable cut, and the editor must therefore either find a cutaway, or dissolve from the first piece of action to the second. But, although a dissolve here is useful and better than a jump cut, it is not really the correct use of the optical in question.

Dissolves, like cuts, can contribute to the pace of the action. A cut brings an immediate change of scene and, possibly subconsciously, an immediate audience reaction. A dissolve brings a gradual transition; it can be very gradual if the dissolve is a long one. This alone suggests a circumstance when it is better to mix from scene to scene than to cut. In a slow, dreamy sequence a few mixes may be more suitable than cuts.

Making a film is, in some respects, like writing a book. The film is not divided into chapters and paragraphs but into main and subsidiary sequences. In a book you have punctuation marks and in a film you must also dictate the pace of the proceedings. Dissolves might be considered to mark the end of paragraphs, and fade-outs make excellent full stops at the end of chapters.

Where to mix

There can be no definite rules about when to mix from one scene to the next. A change of location can sometimes call for a dissolve from one location to the other. If you are moving from a location to one which is entirely different either in character or situation a dissolve can sometimes be the most suitable way of making the transition. It really depends on the mood you want to convey. If you want to make the difference between two locations particularly noticeable, a straight cut from one scene to the other will emphasize the point. If, for example, you are going to move from a quiet office scene to a shot of people dancing in a disco, you can dissolve and fade the music up as the dissolve makes one shot merge with the other. Alternatively you can make a straight cut, which will tend to emphasize the contrast between the quiet office and the noisy disco. If you have to pass from a shot of people sunbathing on a beach to a general view of the coast line, using a dissolve might be a nice way of moving from one scene to the next. If scenes are similar, yet not identical, a dissolve can be quite effective.

If a particular character appears in two shots one of which is seen immediately after the other, you may well be able to move from scene to scene with a cut provided, as I have already explained, the action can be matched at the point at which the cut is made. Perhaps, however, the action cannot be matched, or is deliberately different. In one scene perhaps we see a man working in a factory and in the very next scene we see the same man sunbathing on the shore. To cut directly from one scene to the other with the same man in view on both occasions might be confusing. A dissolve might look better. If the man can be seen throughout the first shot but only in the latter part of the second one it may be quite acceptable to use a cut. Perhaps the second shot starts with a general view of the beach showing thousands of people, before the camera pans round to show the man in question soaking up the sun. In a case like tht it would be quite all right to cut from the preceding office scene to that taking place at the seaside. The general view of many people would be acting as a cutaway. You would not therefore, technically, be cutting directly from a shot of a man at one location to another of the same man at an entirely different location. When such changes of scene are quite inevitable you can always use either a cutaway or a dissolve.

Dissolves are still used in the traditional way to denote the passing of time. In its simplest form a dissolve can be used to mix from a shot of a calendar showing the month of January to a view of the same calendar showing the page for December. You cannot directly cut from one shot to the other if the camera's observation point is the same and if the audience is expected to believe that one complete year has passed. A dissolve will work better. Dissolves are quite often used when you are moving from day scenes to night ones. Again, if the location is the same in two consecutive exposures, a dissolve should link them unless you want to make a very deliberate point of the transition.

Dissolves, when carefully prepared, can be very effective, but to ensure the best possible result both exposures must be carefully matched. Scenes which are similar in pictorial composition can often make particularly pleasing dissolves, for one scene appears to become the other with the minimum of variation in density and texture. There are thousands of possible uses for dissolves in almost any kind of film-making and you will find it is quite rewarding to experiment.

Alternative transitions

A dissolve or mix is not the only way of moving from one scene to another. The *wipe* is another accepted method of transition. In a wipe one scene is moved horizontally in one direction and another scene is introduced immediately behind it. The change can be from left to right of screen or from right to left. This method used to be much favoured by newsreel producers.

6

Creating a soundtrack

In an earlier chapter I stressed the importance of ending up with a full and interesting soundtrack. Let us now see how one can be prepared. The objective in producing a soundtrack is to make a harmonious mixture of sync dialogue, sound effects, music and possibly a commentary which complements the visuals and helps to bring the scenes to life. How does a soundtrack originate? Let us briefly consider the different stages involved.

The first step to take is to view the edited picture. You can't really begin to add music or sound effects until you have almost finished editing your picture. If you start before, and begin to build up the different sound-tracks, you will find that every time you alter a cut in the picture you have to make the same cut at the same point in all your different soundtracks. That could involve you in many complications and a lot of extra work. Edit your picture and synchronized dialogue to begin with, and then think about other sounds. Now, look at the picture and make notes of everything you need. Then gather together the materials you have listed. You may find you have some music and sound effects on film, some on tape and probably some on discs. Before you can use any of the effects you need they will have to be transferred to the right gauge of sprocketed magnetic film.

Breaking down sound

When you have had your sound transferred you will have before you a reel of edited picture and a variety of different sounds on sprocketed film. The next thing to do is to break down the newly recorded soundtracks. It is rather like breaking down the rushes all over again only this time you are only dealing with soundtracks. The normal procedure is to run through each reel of sound on either a synchronizer with a track reader or an editing machine. Break out each piece of film containing a sound effect at the end of that particular recording and then rewind the pieces you have detached, each on its own separate roll, or if it is a short length hang it in the bin. Mark the point at which the sound starts and add some kind of identification ('country atmos/traffic/sea wash' and so on) on the head, writing on the cell (shiny) side of the film with a wax pencil.

Building tracks for a mix

Now you can return to the edited picture and start adding your sound. If shot one shows a scene in a city and shot two shows a scene somewhere in the country you look for two of the effects you are planning to use for these scenes. Perhaps you have a background traffic roar for the city and a country atmosphere track for the other view. Using a synchronizer, put the piece of traffic sound opposite the picture of the city scene. Make sure that the sound starts at the same time as the picture. If, however, you want it faded up, it should be started several feet before the picture begins. And cut it level with the picture at the other end, unless you want the sound mixer to blend the city traffic with the sound of the incoming scene. You are now using two parts of the synchronizer. In the front you have your reel of picture, and in the next track you have your city sound. Now in the track behind that place your country atmosphere soundtrack alongside the picture to which it refers. Where the city scene ends and the country scene begins you will want to lose your traffic soundtrack. Thus you splice white spacing on to the end of that particular effect track at the end of the scene to which it refers. Likewise you will not want the country sounds over the shot of the city so the first part of your second soundtrack can be built up with spacing material.

How does the assembly look if you wind through the reel so far? At the beginning, on all three parts of the synchronizer, you will find a piece of leader. The start of a reel must always be identified with a leader. Winding on you come to the first scene: the city. At the same point as the city scene cuts in on the picture, the sound for it cuts in on the first of the soundtracks. Meanwhile, spacing continues on the other soundtrack. At the end of that scene the countryside picture begins. At the same point the first soundtrack is spliced to spacing and the spacing on the second soundtrack is spliced to an incoming soundtrack of countryside atmosphere. Build up the backgrounds first. These are the first stages in sound editing. After that you can go through again and, without altering your background tracks, add some more. These, too, must exactly match the edited picture. Using these tracks you can add any special details you want in the scenes. Perhaps a bus passes in the foreground. This can be laid on another track, whilst people talking and walking could be added on another, and so on. When you have finally built up all the soundtracks you need, run through them and make out a *dubbing cue sheet*. This is a sheet to guide the sound mixer. It contains a list of all soundtracks and effects. It also gives the precise footages at which you want them to start or end when they are all mixed together to make one track. With the tracks and cue sheets go into a dubbing theatre and mix your tracks together. You have then finished editing the sound.

Cutting sync sound scenes

If you are only handling sequences of synchronized sound you will have few editing problems. Once the rushes have been synchronized all you have to do is to put the scenes together in the right order, cutting in the most suitable place. An editing machine and a synchronizer with track reader will be most useful for this. First remove the clapper board from the first shot and join on a leader. Now you can run through to the first cutting point. If the script calls for a level cut you can make the cut on an editing machine.

A *level cut* is one where sound and picture are cut at the same point. If, for example, an interviewer is asking someone a question, you can cut from the interviewer to the person who is going to answer the question at almost any point. If the action starts with a shot of the interviewer, with his voice on the soundtrack, you can wait until he finishes speaking. Then cut from his picture, and his soundtrack, to show the person who is answering and hear his comments. Such a cut would be a level cut because sound and picture are cut at the same point. The terms *'straight cut'* and *'editorial cut'* are also used to describe the same situation.

Overlaying sound

When you are cutting an interview or any other sync sound shots, sound and picture do not have to be cut at the same point. If you wish you can cut from the picture of the interviewer to the picture of the person who will answer before he has finished asking his question. Then you will find the cut easier to make on a synchronizer. You simply put the first shot in the synchronizer with sound and picture and wind on to the point where you wish to cut from one view to the other. Mark the action here with a wax pencil. In another track of the synchronizer you now place the second shot with its soundtrack, taking care that the soundtrack comes in after the other one has ended. Mark the points where you are to join the two soundtracks, then wind back to the mark you have already made on the

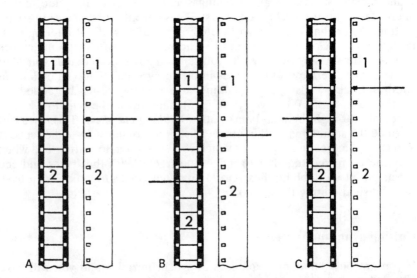

When editing a synchronized interview it is possible to cut sound and picture at the same point (A); or to cut the sound under cover of a cutaway (B); or to overlay part of the track (C).

outgoing picture. Make a similar mark on the incoming action, and cut across. Sound and picture will still be in sync. The only difference is that, when projected, the action will now change from a shot of the interviewer to the other person rather earlier than before. The interviewer's voice will continue over the second shot. A voice carried over in this manner is said to be *overlaid*.

This technique is rather useful to emphasize a particular point. Cuts give emphasis. So if you want to emphasize a particular part of the question, a cut in the picture before the point you wish to outline will make it more noticeable.

The editing of synchronized dialogue is not really difficult. Any kind of interview can be edited in a synchronizer. Mark sync before you cut and you won't have any trouble. These comments, of course, only apply to editing film with a separate magnetic soundtrack.

Cutaways in sync interviews

In this connection the use of cutaway shots for synchronized takes is again worth mentioning. You can cut away at any point, and with the aid of a synchronizer the whole operation only takes a few seconds. Mark the point where you wish to cut out of your first shot and the point where you want to come back to it. Put the shot you are going to use as a cutaway in one of the other tracks of the synchronizer and make corresponding marks. Join the film at the appropriate marks, being sure to make your cut and your splice on the left of the synchronizer to preserve synchronization. The track can be carried through without a cut.

When editing sync scenes you may find that the sound level of different takes varies. Background noises may also vary considerably. Consider, for example, those interviews taking place in that busy street I mentioned earlier. The volume of traffic will never be the same at the end of one interview and at the start of another. Any cuts made in the track between different snatches of dialogue will therefore need improvement. To overcome this, further soundtracks must be added and the different tracks mixed together.

Preserving sync throughout

Some films, as I have already pointed out, are photographed without any synchronized sound. Others have some sync takes and a number of other mute ones. In cases like this, where only part of the film is shot with synchronized sound, when you are editing the sync tracks must be built up with spacing so that synchronization is preserved from the head of the roll. If, again for the sake of an example, your film starts and ends with a synchronized dialogue sequence, spacing should be joined to the end of the first sequence. It should be carried through to the start of the last sequence, where the incoming magnetic track can be joined to it. Both interviews will then be in synchronization with the action to which they refer from the start of the reel. Sound for the intervening scenes will have to be provided, and it is then that sound editing really becomes an interesting task.

Non-sync sound

First you must collect the necessary raw materials. Apart from synchronized dialogue, you will be concerned with three main kinds of additional sound. *Commentary* is the first of the three, *music* the second, and *sound effects* the third. All three are vital to the success of most films, although music is dispensable for some kinds of production. A film with commentary alone will quickly become boring. A film with sound effects alone or with music from beginning to end may need some kind of explanation even if it is only an introduction or summary. The more detailed your soundtrack is the more interesting the finished film is likely to be.

In the course of production the sound recordist may have recorded a number of wild tracks. They will probably be sound effects, but there may also be unsynchronized dialogue, perhaps for use in a crowd scene or some similar gathering where dialogue needs to be audible over background hubbub. Other sound effects are, of course, needed and you will have either to arrange for them to be specially recorded or obtain them from sound effects libraries which may have suitable recordings on disk or on tape. So how do you locate and use the sounds you need?

Ordering sound effects

First wind through the cutting copy and identify the sound effects you need. Make a list, and be sure it is a detailed one. List precisely the effects you require, and note the length of the shots so you can calculate how much you want to use.

The need to be precise cannot be over emphasized. I remember one editor who telephoned a sound effects library and asked for a church bell recording to be delivered. Around fifty records were sent to him and he found himself half buried in recordings of bells of every kind from small country churches to Italian cathedrals! He should, of course, have stated that he wanted a church bell for use with a church in a county town centre.

This need to specify exactly what you want applies equally well to all kinds of sound effect. It is quite useless simply asking for a car effect. You must be much more specific. Is it a sports car or a saloon? What is the make and approximate year of manufacture? Is it going forwards or backwards and at what speed? Is there a visible gear change in the course of the shot? Does the shot include someone switching on and starting the engine or someone braking and turning it off? These are only a few of the questions you must ask yourself before ordering sound effects. If you think it is all unnecessary, listen to a soundtrack of a modern sports car over a picture of a modern saloon and see how absurd the sound is. That is an exaggerated example, but it is very easy to make far more subtle mistakes. Perhaps you are not an expert on cars, but try to get it right because someone in the audience probably is.

When you look at the cutting copy, think carefully of all the effects you will need for each shot. A good soundtrack is made up of a number of different sound effects. Take, for example, a shot of traffic passing through a main thoroughfare. The shot includes views of three cars and a bus passing the camera. To complete this soundtrack correctly, the sound of these cars and the bus should be reconstructed. Behind them, you will need a background atmosphere track of the general hubbub of the main road. A further track with a few motor horns could be added to give extra detail, and a newsvendor's voice would add a little more realism.

When you have chosen the main effects, concentrate on the detailed ones. Look at the footsteps of leading characters appearing in the action. They, too, should be audible, and suitable sound to use must be recorded. These sounds can be obtained from sound libraries, or recorded specially for the production in question. Note the kind of surface the character is walking on. If it is a hard stone surface or a pavement the sound will be different from a gravel path or lino.

There are several ways of reproducing footsteps. Time permitting, it is far better to record them at the time of shooting and then match them to the action in the course of editing. Alternatively, they can be done live to picture. The cutting copy is projected on a dubbing theatre screen and someone recreates the footsteps on a specially prepared surface matching the one in the picture. This method of working is known as *post-synchronizing*. When films are dubbed in different languages similar techniques are used. You need to be an expert to achieve acceptable results without wasting a great deal of time. Other effects, like cups being placed on tables and cigarette lighters being lit, can be done live to picture in a suitable recording theatre, but here again it is better to list the required sounds and shoot them wild, then match the effect to the action. Effects of this kind, when done live to picture, are known as *spot effects*.

Cheated sound effects

You may not always be able to find the exact sound you are looking for. Lack of time or money may oblige you to find some alternative. Occasionally you may find something better than you were originally looking for.

I remember spending a considerable amount of time trying to find a suitable effect for a very old boat chugging into a Scottish harbour. I listened to every boat sound I could obtain but they did not sound right. Then I came across a tape recording labelled '25 hp horizontal sewage pump'. Out of curiosity I played it. It was recorded at seven-and-a-half inches per second. I ran the tape at three-and-a-quarter inches per second and the sound was just what I wanted.

On another occasion I wanted to reproduce the noise of gravel being tipped into an empty lorry. There are, of course, hundreds of good recordings of this effect, but at that time I hadn't got one of them. As the film was wanted in a hurry I had to pick up the sound from other materials. I actually used a recording of the Niagara Falls, again playing it at the wrong speed, and fading it up and down as the gravel was tipped in and as the lorry filled to capacity. It sounded splendid!

So, when you are choosing your sound effects, if you cannot find exactly what you need use your imagination. Think not only of the obvious ones, but of those less evident. Even if a particular sound cannot be directly connected with anything visible in the picture, it can lend much to the atmosphere of a scene. Shots of a pond call for some kind of exterior atmosphere, but the scene is greatly enhanced with a few suitable bird noises. A distant train has often been used to impart character to a scene. There is really no such thing as complete silence. Every location has its own atmosphere and even in a carpeted room rustles of clothing can be easily heard. Anyone who doubts the value of sound should make an effort to see 'Listen to Britain', a wartime documentary which, although rather slow by present-day standards, conveys its message almost entirely by using authentic sounds.

Selecting music

In addition to sound effects you will also need music. If the choice of music is left to you, choose something which is really suitable. Check the copyright–make certain before you use it that it is clearable for the areas in which you want to show the finished film. Be sure, too, that it is clearable at a price the producers of the film can afford. This is by no means always the case. The cost of clearing music, like that of using library material, is assessed by considering the amount of music used and the type of audience the finished film is to be shown to.

Perhaps you do not want to use classical or popular music recorded by companies marketing their records through the usual outlets. You may decide to use 'mood' recordings produced by companies specializing in the production of recordings which are internationally clearable and which are designed for film and television users. Most mood music publishers can provide a catalogue listing the tapes and discs they are able to supply. They are normally classified by types of music and the variety of different kinds available is quite astonishing. Anyone wanting a piece of music to add dramatic impact to a scene can choose from several hundred different recordings of what are known as dramatic *stings*. Lighthearted curtain raisers and short musical links for every kind of mood are also plentiful, and the selection of longer pieces is really enormous. Whatever the instrument, and whatever the nationality, somewhere it is usually possible to obtain a mood music recording. Study the different publishers' catalogues, and then ask them to supply the recordings you want to hear. You may be charged with the cost of all the records supplied, but you will only be charged royalties on the recordings you actually use in the finished film.

7

The mechanics of editing sound

Sound transfers

Before the business of sound editing can begin, all your chosen music and sound effects recordings must be re-recorded on perforated magnetic film. The sound can then be handled alongside the visuals. Most dubbing theatres have allied transfer facilities and so do some laboratories. You can take your discs and tapes along and have them transferred to either 16 mm or 35 mm magnetic film, depending on which you prefer to edit and which your editing machine can cope with. Transfer time is quite expensive. It is worth working out in advance the footages of the tape you want to transfer and the exact part of the disc you want to re-record.

Tell the transfer recordist exactly what you need. Let him know if you want to record on 16 mm and the speed at which you want to re-record. For most purposes this will be 24 frames per second, but for television in some countries, including Great Britain, 25 fps is standard. You might think one frame would make no difference, but it does. Listen to any familiar piece of music at 24 fps and then play the 24 fps recording at 25 fps and listen carefully: you will notice a change.

It is possible to record on one of two positions on 16 mm. Some stock is *centre-track*, recording in the middle of the film. Others are *edge-track*, recording on the edge opposite the sprocket holes. Because centre-track recordings cover a larger area the sound quality is usually better than on edge, and they are thus more widely used. Most editing machines can cope with both types, but on some older machines you may need to change the magnetic sound head or switch it round when moving from one to another.

On 35 mm film, it is again possible to have two different tracks–one on each side of the stock–and, unlike 16 mm, on 35 mm you can use both tracks. It is quite normal to record one track on one direction on one side of the stock and another in the other direction near the opposite set of perforations.

Ordering transfers

If you cannot yourself attend a transfer session, be sure you send really detailed instructions to guide the recordist. State the speed of the

recording you wish to transfer. If it is a disc, tell him which band to
re-record and how much of it is wanted, and state whether you are talking
about the front or the back of the record. It is no use giving a record
number and saying band two. He wants to know what side. Some record
companies use the same number for both sides of a reording so it pays to
give the title or a brief description as well. If you are sending tape for
transfer, again state the speed. Is it full track or half track, and at what
speed was it recorded?

You should normally transfer rather more sound than is needed to cover
the actual scene depicted on the film. When the soundtracks are mixed
together in a dubbing theatre, an overlap may be needed to provide
smooth transition from one sound to another. In fact it always pays to
record more sound than you ever expect to need. Some sounds, of course,
do not need to be lifted to the full length of the shot. If you have a very
long street scene you may need to re-record the actual sounds of any
vehicles passing near to the camera. You will also need a background
traffic effect of a general roar, but you will not need to record enough of it
to cover the whole scene. You should transfer your background sound to
magnetic (perforated) film in the normal way. You can then *loop* a section
of the sound you have lifted so that the same piece runs round and round
throughout the entire scene.

Sound loops

When recording sound which you intend to loop, take care not to record
anything which makes the fact that you are using a loop abundantly
obvious. If you have one outstanding effect it will be noticed every time the
loop goes round. In the case of the traffic loop, for example, avoid any
obvious motor horns or voices. If you are looping a party atmos listen for
any distinctive laughs or coughs and make the loop long enough to avoid
them being obviously repetitive. All you have to do is to record a length of
the effect you want to loop. Pick two points where the recording levels are
identical and diagonally splice the two points end to end to form a loop.
Make sure before you join the ends together that the loop is not twisted.
Take care also to splice at a point where there is only background
atmosphere, where the join will be not be noticed, not in the middle of a
specific effect. Loops can save a great deal of trouble. Their main use is in
providing background atmospheres. Audience-murmur loops for theatre
scenes, factory-noise loops for industry, countryside loops for open-air
scenes are all useful. The main characteristic of a loop should be overall
atmosphere, lacking specific detail of any kind. If you want detail, provide
it on your other soundtracks and use a loop to back it up. In the case of a
tractor drawing up in the middle of a field, for example, the tractor arriving
should be laid on one soundtrack. The tractor cab doors opening and being
shut should be laid on another. A background countryside atmosphere of
wind and birds can then be laid as another track or provided by a loop. The
same principle applies in a factory. If you are showing a machine, put the
actual effect of the machine on a separate soundtrack. Use a background
factory atmosphere loop to back it up. You will be surprised how a good

loop will improve the authenticity of a scene, and, of course, it also saves time and stock costs.

Recording a commentary

Before you can start editing your music and effects and matching them to the action, you may have to record and edit the film commentary. Sometimes you may not be able to record it at this stage, for the producers may wish to write it when the film is completely finished and add it live in the course of dubbing. This can be done, but the course is not really recommended.

It is far better to record your commentary at the same time as the music and effects and then adjust the picture to match it exactly. The advantages are numerous. You can be sure that the commentary will be exactly where you want it to be. You will also save time in the dubbing theatre, because few commentators get a live commentary right first time. You can waste a lot of time going back and forth with the picture until the commentator gives the required performance at the right point.

Brief the commentator beforehand and if you can, give him the script at least a day before you are due to record it. When he has studied it, listen to what he has to say about it. He may ask for the wording of some passages to be altered slightly. Do not say 'No' on principle. He knows what he can read without sounding awkward and, if wording can be altered to suit him without changing the meaning, it may be worth making the alteration. Tell him if there are any particular words you would like him to emphasize and where you want him to pause, and run over any names or technical terms before you start to record. Make sure that where there is to be a gap in the film commentary, he pauses for long enough to enable you to cut the track without cutting an echo of his voice or a breath being drawn. If you take those simple precautions you should have no trouble. When the recording session is completed you will have several reels of unedited commentary, music and sound effects. With those in hand you can return to the cutting-room.

Laying a commentary track

Now you can look at your cutting copy once again. Taking the first part of the commentary you have recorded, and subsequently broken down into sentences or paragraphs, thread the picture and sound together on an editing machine or a synchronizer. You can now adjust the two until the commentary comes in at the right point. Run back to the start of the commentary and splice on a leader or spacing, making sure that some kind of start mark occurs at exactly the same point as the start mark on the picture. When you have tidied up the start of the commentary track in this manner, you can again return to the end of the first shot. Perhaps, now you have the commentary to cover the shot, you will find that in the first rough assembly you have left the action too long. Now is the time to shorten it, until the commentary fits exactly. Alternatively you may find the commentary is too short. In that case you have two alternatives. You can either extend the spacing on the start of the track so that the commentary starts rather later, or divide the commentary into two parts, assuming, of course, that there is a point where the sentence or sentences can be divided without making nonsense of the dialogue. If there is such a point you simply mark it on the cellulose side of the track with a wax pencil. Making sure that you do not lose synchronization by cutting on the left-hand side of the synchronizer or editing machine (before the gate and not after it), you simply splice spacing on to the track at the end of the first sentence. The spacing can be carried through up to the point where you want the second sentence to begin. The second piece of track can then be joined to it.

All soundtracks consist of a considerable amount of spacing as well as magnetic sound stock and the practice of building up sound in this manner is standard practice. Some sequences may not have any commentary at all. For those you will again need to build up the commentary track with spacing. Working this way you will ensure that the commentary exactly matches the appropriate shots and remains in perfect synchronization from one end of the reel to the other.

Checking commentary sync

Building up a commentary track alongside the edited picture by using spacing in the way I have just described is known as *laying* a commentary track. The commentary track will be the first of several tracks you will have to lay in the course of editing. By the time you have finished laying the commentary you should have a reel of edited picture very near in length to the ultimate length of the film, for in fitting commentary to picture and picture to commentary many adjustments will have to be made. When you have finished the track, it is well worth winding back to the start of the reel and then projecting it again. Watch each cut carefully to make sure it is still acceptable. Check the action and the commentary against the script to make sure that they are exactly what is required. When you are sure it is right, put the commentary away in a can and rewind the action.

Joining magnetic tracks

When you join spacing to magnetic sound it is worth noting that the type of splice required is slightly different from that normally required when joining two pieces of film together. In the first place, you do not join the cellulose side of one piece of film to the emulsion side of the other, as usual. For a normal film splice you scrape the emulsion side of one of the two pieces of film, and then, after applying film cement, bring the cell side of another piece of film in contact with the wet cement. When the process has been completed both pieces of film are the same way round, emulsion up, in the splicer. When splicing spacing to magnetic, however, the principle is different. Here, unless you are using specially toughened spacing designed only for use with magnetic film, it is best to join cellulose to cellulose: the shiny side of the soundtrack should be brought in contact with the shiny side of the spacing. You do not even need to scrape the splice. Just apply cement, or if you are splicing with tape draw the tape across in the normal manner. The reason for making this kind of splice is a good one. Magnetic soundheads are tough pieces of equipment and they tend to scrape the emulsion off white spacing and clog themselves up, thus impairing the quality of sound reproduction. The cellulose side of spacing is harder than the emulsion side and is therefore not damaged in the same manner. The spacing can pass over the heads without clogging them and the soundhead will thus be able to reproduce the magnetic sound recorded on the track which is intercut with spacing in the best way possible. It is a small point, but one worth remembering. When splicing magnetic to spacing splice cellulose to cellulose. When joining magnetic to magnetic splice in the normal manner.

Laying spot effects

When laying sound effects you will again use a synchronizer. First wind through the cutting copy and mark the exact spot where each sound is required. Draw a cross for each footstep at the point where the foot actually touches the ground. Mark a cross where a car door is opened and where it actually bangs closed and so on. Then rewind the film and put it back in the front of the synchronizer. In one track you will need a roll of spacing. Mark a start mark on it level with the start mark on the picture and wind down to the first mark on your print. A glance at the print reminds you that this is where you want the sound of a car door opening. Find the effect in the bin and check it by playing it on the editing machine. Mark the exact frame where the noise of the door opening starts and finishes. You can then return to the synchronizer and mark the spacing at a point level with the cross you put on the cutting copy. Join the mark on the spacing to the mark indicating the start of the effect on the magnetic soundtrack. At the other end of the effect you can again splice on white spacing, taking care to splice it the right way round, cellulose to cellulose.

You can now wind the film through the synchronizer. If you have cut and joined at the right point the magnetic stock should come opposite the mark on your cutting print and you should be able to hear the car door opening and check that it is in sync. If it sounds all right you can wind down to the next mark, where the car door closes. Here again you need to mark the spacing before selecting the effect and slotting it in in the same manner. This is the standard procedure for laying all spot effects – effects which have to be accurately synchronized. When you reach the end of the film take the cutting copy action and the reel of magnetic track intercut with spacing out of the synchronizer and rewind them. If you want to check your work you can now run the picture and track on an editing machine. If you have marked up the cutting copy and the sound effects accurately and have joined with care you should not find there is any need to change what you have done, but if you have made an error it is better to discover it now and not in the dubbing theatre, where delays can prove costly. If you find a few of the effects need moving a frame or more one way or the other you can make the necessary adjustments. When you are sure everything is right you

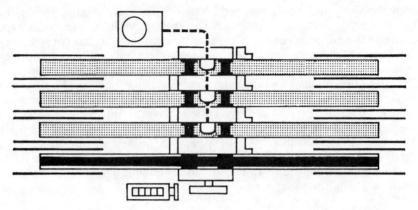

The synchronizer used for laying soundtracks. At the bottom is a footage counter. The picture runs through the track nearest to it. In the three adjacent tracks run separate magnetic tracks. Under each of these tracks is a magnetic soundhead, connected to an amplifier at the back of the sync bench.

can identify the start of the reel with the title of the film and the words 'Effect 1', or 'Fx 1', as it is usually abbreviated. You can then again turn your attention to the action.

So far, you have laid a commentary track and a track of footsteps, car doors and other spot effects. That is good start but is by no means a detailed soundtrack. Now you can wind through and complete the job. Again a synchronizer will be the most suitable equipment to use but you can use an editing machine if a synchronizer is not available. When track laying it is easier to be frame-accurate using a synchronizer. It is also quicker. Many of the sound effects you still need are not spot effects. They last longer than the few seconds required for a footstep or a door. You may be able to use loops for some of the sounds. The remainder will form the basis of your other effects soundtracks. Let us look at the composition of these different tracks in terms of a definite situation.

Planned effects

Imagine we have a dock scene where crates of materials are being loaded on to a ship by a crane. The crates are being moved into position by a fork-lift truck, which puts them down at a point from which a crane picks them up and carries them away to the ship's hold. The script calls for several shots.

The first shot starts as a long-shot showing the whole of the ship, making the fork-lift truck very small and insignificant. The script indicates that the field of view tightens as the camera zooms in to the centre of the ship and the fork-lift truck standing alongside it. In the second shot, we see only the fork-lift truck. It lifts a pile of crates into position. The third shot is a wider view. It shows the overhead crane coming down to lift up the crates and carry them out of shot. We then go back to the fork-lift truck, which is reloading. What does this mean in the terms of soundtracks? The script also shows that there is no dialogue or commentary. The scene depends only on authentic sounds for its effectiveness. A background docks atmosphere loop will do much to create the atmosphere of the surroundings. Distant cranes, the sea, possibly an engine shunting waggons far away, would be suitable material. That is a start. Now for the other effects.

On the first shot, both the crane and the fork-lift truck are very insignificant, but they could both be audible. In the course of the shot, the camera tightens the angle of vision to make them more obvious. They should be audible, for the sound mixer will want to fade up the sounds as the camera moves into a closer view. You should therefore lay on one track the effect of a fork-lift truck and on the other the noise of the crane. Make sure you match the truck exactly to the action you are watching. Where the fork-lift truck moves off have the appropriate sound, and make sure the effect finishes when the truck has stopped moving. Likewise, watch the movements of the crane.

In the second shot we can only see the fork-lift truck. Obviously the audience will expect to hear the noise it is making, but possibly subconsciously they will also want to continue to hear the crane in the background. If the crane cuts out at the end of the previous shot they will think it has ceased to work. Carry the sound through.

To sum up, then: on the first track you should have the fork-lift truck, on the second the crane, and on the third the noise of the crates being lowered to the ship's hold. A background loop will fill in the details. The third shot features the crane. This time you will need to carry the sound of the fork-lift truck through, even though it is not visible. When all the tracks are mixed together you will be surprised to find how authentic they sound.

Sound cuts

Because the action in a scene comes to an end, you do not necessarily have to end the sound associated with it. Indeed, with skill and imagination one sound can be used to lead into a scene or to help smooth the transition from one scene to another. It is always wise to allow more sound than you actually need, for the sound mixer will be able to lose the part you do not want and a good overlap at the beginning and end of each effect can be useful. That does not, of course, usually apply where you are cutting from a scene filmed at one location to another shot somewhere entirely different. Then, cut the track, unless you wish to mix the outgoing and incoming sounds together.

Some sounds need to be eased in and out. If you are cutting from a shot of a jet plane landing on an airport runway to a scene in the interior of an airport lounge a straight sound cut from the very noisy jet to the relatively quiet interior might not sound right. It would be better to merge the two sounds together by mixing as quickly or as slowly as you wish from one to the other. Lay one of the effects on one track, carrying it on for several feet past the picture cut, and put the other sound on another, bringing it in several feet before the change of scene. The sound mixer can then ease one out and the other in and the abrupt effect of a straight cut will be avoided. If you want the change to be almost instantaneous that can still be done, but if the outgoing noisy sound is faded, however quickly, it will sound better than if it is cut off suddenly with a quiet sound coming in in the next shot.

This is a general rule, and, as with all rules, there are exceptions. If you are cutting a dramatic sequence showing someone racing through the airport reception hall, intercut with shots of a plane taxiing and taking off, you might well enhance the drama of the situation by cutting from one sound effect to the other. A straight cut would be more dramatic and would emphasize the difference in location.

Carrying sound through

You will find there are occasions when you need to carry sound through so that it can continue to be heard after the picture it refers to has disappeared. This need is not always understood by inexperienced film-makers. Perhaps you have seen a film made by someone who thinks the audience wants to hear only what it can see. Consequently when a bus comes into the shot the soundtrack is suddenly filled with the noise of its engine. The moment it passes out of shot, the sound cuts off sharply. The overall effect is uncomfortable to watch and unrealistic. The correct course to take is to find out where the bus comes into the shot and then run back a few feet. Start laying the noise of the bus several feet before it enters the picture. When it goes out of shot, carry the sound on for a few feet past the cut. When you make out cue sheets for dubbing, specify the point where the mixer should start fading up the sound effect, the place where it should be at full volume, and the place where it should start to fade out. The sound will then come and go smoothly just as it would if you stood in the street shown in the picture and listened to a bus going by. The sound will be natural and the scene will be easier to watch.

Laying music tracks

In most films where music is used it is required only as a background. It should never be used to replace sound effects. Some film-makers are lazy and feel that if they lay a few pieces of music over the scenes they need not be bothered with sound effects. They lose many opportunities, for sound effects are excellent on their own, but can also do much to augment music when heard behind it. If you want to make a feature of the music you may decide to match your picture cuts to the beat of the music. Cutting to music can be very effective. All you have to do is run through the mag of the music you want to use and mark the beats of the music on the back of the track. You can then cut the pictures to match the beats.

When you lay music, find out first of all where you want it to begin and to end. If you know where you want the end to be, wind the picture on to that point on the editing machine or in a synchronizer. Put the end of the music track you want to use opposite the point where you wish it to end on the picture. Now wind back and listen to it. See if it fits well and if it comes in at the right place. If it doesn't, see if it can be faded up later without coming in at an unsuitable place.

Making short music longer

Sometimes you find the music chosen is too short for the scene. If you are lucky you may be able to join two pieces of the music together in a manner which will not be detected by anyone but the composer. More probably you will find such a cut very noticeable. If so, you must record the piece of music you want to use twice. Lay the start of the first recording at the point where you want it to start. Then proceed to the point the music section should end. On another track lay the other music recording back from the point at which you wish the sound to finish. Somewhere the two recordings will overlap. Now if you lay the music skilfully enough, you may sometimes be able to mix from one track to the other in the course of the music. Certain kinds of music are more suitable than others. Percussion pieces are favourites for this kind of work. If you cannot mix across in an unnotice-able fashion, you will have to fade out the first piece and fade in the second. Pick a point where the fade-out and fade-in can be covered by sound effects or commentary and few people will notice. The audience will only be aware that the music comes in at a suitable point and goes out at another. The sound effects, if skilfully chosen and laid, will disguise the transition from one recording to another.

Dubbing theatre equipment

When you have laid all your tracks you can arrange for them to be mixed together to make one composite track – the final mix master. That will

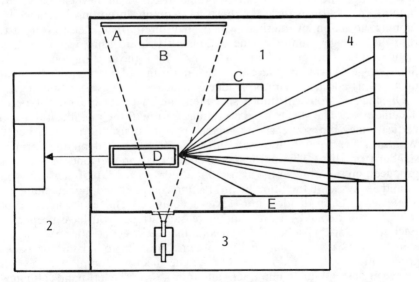

Room 1: soundproofed theatre. (A) Screen. (B) Footage counter. (C) Gramophone turntables. (D) Mixing console manned by sound mixer. (E) Commentary box. Room 2: sound recording room, containing recording equipment. Room 3: projection room, containing projector locked in sync with recorder and reproducers. Room 4: sound reproduction room, containing series of sound reproducers.

have to be done in a film dubbing theatre. In its simplest form the equipment you will find in a dubbing theatre consists of a projector which is electronically locked to run in synchronization with a number of 16 mm or 35 mm sound reproducing machines and one recorder.

All the machines will run at the same speed forwards or backwards and remain in sync, so if the sound mixer misses a cue you can stop and run back to the start of the scene and re-record without having to go right back to the head of the roll. The sound output of the reproducers is fed through a console containing numerous controls designed to alter the quality of each individual soundtrack as required. The console also contains a series of volume controls which make it possible to fade each track in and out or mix from one to the other as and when required. The whole operation is controlled by a sound mixer who sits at the console, watching the projected picture of your cutting copy on a screen in front of him. Underneath the screen is a footage counter. As the film moves on, the footage counter records its progress. In front of him, the mixer also has a detailed *cue sheet*. It tells him everything he needs to know about the film he is mixing. You will have to prepare that sheet when you are editing, so let's see what it must show and how it should be laid out.

Dubbing cue sheets

The main purpose of a cue sheet is to tell the mixer exactly what is on each soundtrack and to specify the point at which each sound starts and ends. You must also specify how you want it to come in and go out. Do you want it faded in or out, or mixed to another track, or just left to cut out as you have laid it? The cue sheet can be prepared either on a synchronizer, by running the action with all of the tracks, or on an editing machine, by running the action several times with each different track. Before you start, zero the footage counter on the equipment you are using when the first picture on the start of the film first begins. This is the starting point of your film footage. Always measure from the first frame of picture (unless sound precedes it) and not from the leader or spacing on the very beginning.

On page 95 you will find a specimen cue sheet for a normal type of documentary. The sheets have no standard format—the one illustrated is a vertical one, but some sound mixers prefer to use horizontal sheets. Whatever the format, the basic information contained on the form is standard practice. This particular cue sheet is for reel one of a film I produced on the work of the artist John Piper. At the top of the sheet you should always write the title, the production company and the reel number. The cue sheet is divided into several columns. The exact number of columns will depend on the number of soundtracks you have prepared. Each soundtrack must have its own column and the action must also have a column of its own. Additionally, columns must be found for the background loops you intend to use. On the cue sheet for John Piper you will see we are using four 16 mm tracks and four loops. The left-hand column is devoted to the action. The first of the soundtracks consists only of commentary. The others are built up of a mixture of music and effects. You should never put commentary on more than one track and, where possible, it is not a bad idea to keep music on a track by itself.

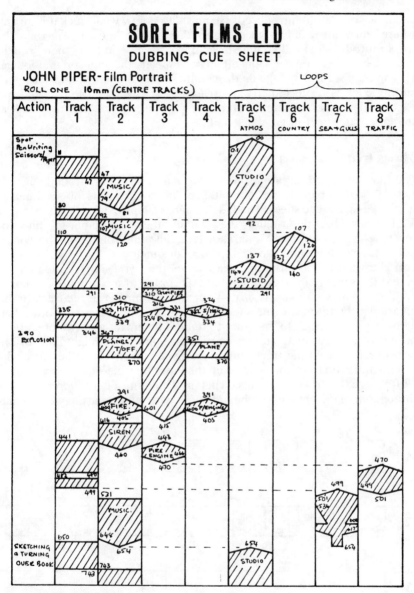

Example of a dubbing cue sheet for a documentary film, using a vertical layout.

Cueing sound transitions

There are three main ways of putting two soundtracks together. You can cut from one to the other, you can fade one out and fade in the other, or you can mix the two sounds together, gradually losing one and at the same time increasing the volume of the other. Each of these ways has to be specified on a cue sheet–you have to let the mixer see at a glance exactly what you want him to do. He must know where each sound must come in, and how you want it introduced. He must also know what track it is on and where you want it faded out or boosted. He must know if you want the track reproduced at full volume or held low for a period and then brought up. The cue sheet must tell him all this and specify the appropriate footage. He can then see the footage on the counter under the screen on which your cutting copy is projected. By referring to the cue sheet he can find out exactly what you want him to do at every given point. Let us now look at the Piper cue sheet in greater detail.

Mixing from a cue sheet

The film starts with an atmosphere loop – a general background which is faded in at 0 feet and has reached full volume by 1 ft. This loop is noted as track five on the cue sheet. The fade-in sign is simply a large inverted letter V. The narrowest point marks the start and the widest point the finish of the fade-in. An upright V marks a fade-out: full volume at the widest point, fading to nothing where the two sides meet.

If you want to mix from one track to another, you simply fade out one and at the same point fade in another. This kind of mix from one track to another is known as a *cross-mix*. If you are not mixing to the track in the adjacent column on the cue sheet, it is worth putting a small dotted line across from one track to the other to remind the mixer that two operations have to be performed at that particular point. A straight line drawn horizontally across the track simply marks a cut. At 11 ft, therefore, the commentary, on track one, cuts in on the Piper film cue sheet. It cuts out at 47 ft where, on track two, music cuts in. The atmosphere loop continues throughout. Track two has to be faded out with a fade starting at 79 ft and

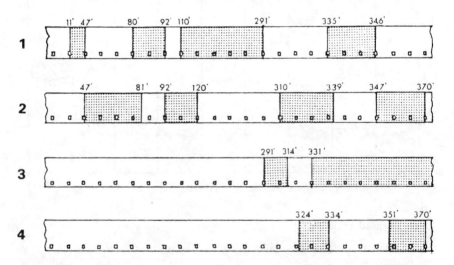

Composition of soundtracks for *John Piper: a Film Portrait*. (See also the dubbing cue sheet for the film.) Note particularly how tracks are cut in *before* fades are needed. Fades and dissolves on the cue sheet appear as cuts on the actual tracks, though the cuts are always overlapping the required footages. Fading and mixing are done in the dubbing process, but tracks must be suitably overlapped beforehand.

ending at 81 ft. Commentary cuts in on track one at 80 ft and out at 92 ft where music again replaces it on track two. At 107 ft there is a cross mix out of the music on track 2 into a loop of country atmos. At 137 ft there is a cross mix from that loop into another loop of studio atmos. A war sequence begins at 291 ft. It is built up on several different tracks, all of which are, on several occasions, open at the same time. The battle begins with gunfire, on track three at 291 ft. This cross mixes at 310 ft to track two, where Hitler's voice takes over. This is augmented by a series of planes, which are faded up at 331 ft, to reach full volume by 334 ft. Hitler's voice starts to fade out one foot earlier but does not disappear completely until 339 ft. At the same time as the Hitler speech, on track four a crowd chanting 'Sieg Heil!' is faded up at 324 feet and cross-mixed out to track three (the planes) at 334 ft. The main plane noises continue on track three but at 347 ft we have a more detailed shot which includes some planes taking off. These effects have been laid in the synchronizer to cut in at 347 ft and cut out at 370 ft on track two. At 351 ft there is another prominent plane in shot, and sound for this has been laid at 351 ft on track four. At this point tracks two, three and four are all open. And so it goes on until the end of the reel.

At the foot of the last cue-sheet for each reel is marked the end footage of the reel, so that the mixer knows how much stock he needs to record on. The recording he makes is your final mix master soundtrack. From it, you will be able to produce either magnetic soundtracks of comparable quality or materials for making prints with combined optical sound (comopt).

Pre-mixing

Sometimes the sound mixer will not want to mix all your soundtracks at once. Perhaps, in the case of a major production, there are not enough reproducing soundheads to cope with all the tracks you want to contribute to the finished final mix. Possibly too many things are happening at a particular point of the film. In cases like this, the mixer will arrange to make a pre-mix. This simply means that he will mix some of the tracks together first and then reproduce the partially mixed recording with the remaining tracks, mixing all together.

It is often best to pre-mix all music and effects recordings before adding commentary. If you are planning to make foreign-language versions of the film, it is, of course, essential, for a separate *music and effects track* (known as an *M and E*) is vital for language dubbing. It should be free of everything but synchronized dialogue, music and effects. Synchronized dialogue, not commentary spoken out of view of the camera, should be kept on an M and E unless you are planing to re-voice it in the appropriate language.

Minimizing dubbing costs

Before you take your film into a dubbing theatre, check again that everything really is ready for the dub. Have you clearly marked the reel number and the track number on the head of each reel? If you turn up with a reel of picture and five unidentified reels of magnetic track you will waste a great deal of time finding out which are the tracks referred to in your cue sheets. Time in a dubbing theatre can be expensive. Above all, come with everything you need. Nothing is more frustrating than sitting round waiting for one loop or page of a cue sheet which you have accidentally forgotten to bring along. And do make sure the tracks are in sync before you arrive. Moving tracks around to try and synchronize them in a dubbing theatre is always unsatisfactory and very time-consuming. Make sure that there is enough blank leader film on the head of each roll to lace the machines up with and plenty of blank on the end so the film does not run out of sync immediately the last effect has passed through. Again they are small points but if you ignore them they can cost money you will otherwise not need to spend.

Adding effects in a dub

You may sometimes find you have to dub a film in a hurry. Having worked for a number of years in television I know in how much of a rush some films have to be prepared. You sometimes have only a couple of hours to put together five or ten minutes of film, dub it and have it ready for showing. On occasions like that, it may be impossible to lay all the soundtracks you require. You may be able to use discs and tapes to help you out, for a sound mixer can often drop in sound effects recordings at a precise footage, although he will want to be cued. Loops, too, may help in an emergency.

Many effects can be done 'live to picture' in the dubbing theatre, although this method should only be used by people with experience. Footsteps and other spot effects can often be reproduced quite satisfactorily in front of a microphone in the dubbing theatre, although you must take care to match the perspective and acoustics of the actual picture being projected. Run through the cutting copy carefully beforehand. Note the footages at which effects are required and the precise nature of the effects. Get the 'props' you will need together and have a rehearsal with the picture. If you are doing footsteps note carefully the type of surface people are walking on. Wood and stone are really quite easy. A few planks nailed together are adequate for mocking up floorboard effects, and flagstones are suitable for any concrete surface. Sand is another easy effect to recreate. It is really easiest to put a small amount of sand in a sack and dampen it slightly. Fold over the top of the sack so that none of the sand is actually visible, and make the footsteps required by prodding the sack with your fingers. If the movement is sharp and clear-cut it will sound exactly like footsteps on sand or on snow, but be careful to match the exact movements of people on the screen.

Spot effects are far better recorded in advance of dubbing and laid on one of your soundtracks. But when this is impossible, cigarette lighters, glass clinks and ordinary clothes rustles can all be done quite satisfactoirly in a dubbing theatre by experienced people. Do not underestimate the small points like clothes rustles–they all lend something to a scene and it is

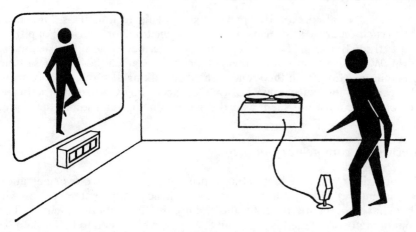

When adding sound effects to picture in a dubbing theatre, the effects man watches a screen and the footage counter underneath it, and repeats the required actions, which are recorded on a recorder running in sync with the projected picture.

always a good idea to put in relevant detail. A few years ago I spent several weeks supervising the dubbing of the science fiction TV series 'Doctor Who'. For copyright reasons at that time the original soundtracks could not be used in certain territories so we had to start from scratch and re-create all the sounds involved in 52 reasonably specialist TV programmes. It took several weeks and was great fun, and we used the techniques I have described above.

Re-voicing dialogue

Sometimes the voices of synchronized dialogue sequences will be unusable. Possibly they are recorded in the wrong language for the intended audience. Alternatively, they may have just been badly recorded: background noise may drown the voice of the person who is speaking. In cases like this you will have to re-voice the scenes in question. Either the actor appearing in the scene, or one with a voice which matches the physical characteristics of the person concerned, must first be brought to the dubbing theatre. He must be given details of the script. The film must be broken down beforehand into loops. The actual length of the loop will depend on the amount of dialogue in each scene and how much the actor can cope with. The loops are made up of scenes extracted from the cutting copy, which are joined end to end to run continuously. They are laced on a projector and synchronized with a loop of new magnetic stock. The original sound-track is sometimes run simultaneously and fed through headphones to the actor, who uses it as a guide track. When he hears the dialogue start on the guide track he will start talking, trying to match exactly the lip movements of the action projected in front of him. His performance will be recorded and re-recorded over and over again as the loops revolve, until the voice exactly matches the lip movement on the screen. The loop will then be saved and eventually mixed with an M & E to produce a final mix of the new version. This technique is known as *post-synchronization* – or usually just *post-sync* for short. It is full of pitfalls but extremely useful. I have deliberately described it here in its simplest form. When re-voicing a film always take care to match the acoustics of the scene in question. If in the scene an actor is talking at some distance from the camera, his voice must be lowered accordingly when the action is re-voiced. It must not seem as if the script is being read somewhere else.

Recording commentary to picture

On occasions you may be unable to pre-record your voice-over narration (commentary) and lay it as a separate soundtrack before you mix. You will then have to record it to fit the picture in the dubbing theatre. The commentator will take his cue from footages, which need to be marked on his script as well as visible on the footage counters under the screen and in the commentary recording booth. Let him know when he will have to do his part by cueing him in. You can do this from footages or by switching on a cue light in front of him when you want him to speak.

Before you record anything, make your commentator comfortable and put him at his ease. Show him the film so he knows what it is all about and let him rehearse and go through the script with you until he is quite happy with it. Keep the script flat, preferably in separate sheets of protective plastic, where it will not rustle, and make sure the chair he is sitting on does not creak. If you take these simple precautions you will again be able to save time and money when you dub.

At the end of a dubbing session you will have your edited cutting copy and a final mix master recording of your soundtrack. For the first time all your soundtracks will be on one piece of perforated magnetic film. Now you can return to the cutting room and put the finishing touches to the film you are cutting.

8

Opticals and titles

Let us now turn our attention to the ordering and production of optical effects. We shall consider dissolves first. As I have already mentioned, a *dissolve* consists of a fade-out of one scene and a fade-in of another, superimposed and starting and ending at the same precise point. In the middle of a dissolve one scene should be half faded out and the other half faded in, the exact amount being calculated in frames. It is, of course, perfectly possible to produce fade-ins and -outs in the camera. You simply open or close either the lens stop or a variable shutter at the pace required. A dissolve can also be produced in the camera. You note the exact point where you start to fade out the first scene. Then, without re-exposing, wind the film back to the same point of your required dissolve and start to fade in the second exposure, making sure the overall length of the fade-in does not exceed that of the fade-out of the previous exposure. The two scenes will thus be partially superimposed and, if the work is done with care and precision, an acceptable dissolve should be produced. But this system of camera opticals does have very serious limitations–serious enough in fact to make it impracticable to the professional film-maker.

The biggest problem of all is knowing where you want a dissolve to come. When a film is exposed, it is almost impossible to know exactly at which point you will want to mix from one scene to another. In the case of titles it is all reasonably simple. You know that the first title must last for one length of time, and the second one for another, and can time your dissolve accordingly. When you are shooting live action it is much more difficult to predict the right time to move from one scene to the other. Until the film is edited you may be unable to tell where the best point is. It is far better to leave the whole question of optical effects until you have an edited version of the picture. You can then arrange for a laboratory to produce the correct effects for you. At that stage, you will have the edited cutting copy to help you. You can run through it as many times as you please until you are absolutely certain where you want to dissolve, or to fade in or out. You then simply order the effect required.

Indicating opticals

You must first of all mark the length of the effect on the cellulose side of the cutting copy with a wax pencil. There are accepted ways of marking up different kinds of opticals. For a dissolve you mark a line from one side of the picture at one end of the dissolve, to the opposite side of the picture in the centre of the dissolve (where you have spliced the two shots in the cutting copy) and then back again to the other side to end at the point at which the dissolve is required to end. A fade-out is marked by placing a

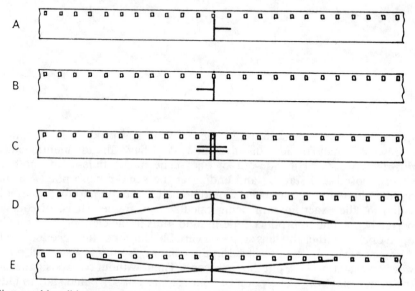

Signs used in editing procedure. (A) Cut: lose right-hand portion. (B) Cut: lose left-hand portion. (C) Carry through: ignore cut. (D) Dissolve (mix). (E) Fade-out; fade-in.

large letter V in the picture. The open part of the letter should start where the fade-out is required to begin, and the base of the letter should mark its end. For a fade-in, the procedure is reversed. A wipe consists solely of one straight line crossing from one side of the picture to the other in the required direction. These signs are internationally understood and require no further explanation. Their presence will guide the negative cutter when he starts to match the master material to your cutting copy. There is a further point to be considered when ordering opticals. To understand this we must first look at how opticals are made.

Production of opticals

As we shall see later, there are two ways of matching negative to a cutting copy. The negative can be made up into two separate rolls, or it can remain in one. If it stays in one, it is made to match the cutting copy precisely. Where there is a splice on the cutting copy there will be a splice on the negative, and scene will match scene and cut will match cut throughout the roll. In the alternative method, the first scene will be put on one roll of negative. If the second scene follows the first with a cut it may also be on the same roll, but if scene one dissolves to scene two, the second shot would be placed on a second roll of negative. The first roll would be carried on throughout the length of the second shot and would be built up with opaque spacing. At the next dissolve the incoming scene would be placed on the first reel and spacing would build up the second. This would be carried on to the end of the film, the negative being built up scene by scene to match the cutting copy on two separate rolls which, when printed together on the same roll of stock, would produce a single print identical in form to the edited cutting copy.

What is the advantage of dividing the negative into two separate rolls and why divide them where one scene dissolves into another? This kind of negative is known as an *A and B roll*; its composition and use are considered later. At this point let us just consider why the reels are changed at dissolves and not necessarily at every scene change. To understand the answer to that you need to remember what has to be done to produce a dissolve if it is done in the camera. You fade out one picture and fade in the other, overlapping the two actions. Now, obviously, in a single roll of negative it is not possible to have two pieces of film physically overlapping each other. You must allow for the overlap by placing your negative on separate rolls. So in an A and B roll master assembly you place the outgoing shot of a dissolve on the first roll. Leave the negative over-length, allowing half as much spare film as the length of the actual optical. On the other negative reel you place the negative of the incoming exposure, this time overlapping the outgoing action by keeping an extra length of film at the beginning of the optical. Again the length required is half the length of the actual effect: for a 40-frame dissolve, 20 extra frames are required in each direction from the centre of the optical, and so on. When the laboratory produce prints from this negative they will start to fade out the outgoing shot on one roll of negative at a given point. They will also fade in reel two at the same point, and the required dissolve will thus be produced on the print.

Opticals from single-roll negatives

We have seen how dissolves can be produced from A and B rolls of negative, but this does not mean that optical effects cannot be produced when negatives are cut in single rolls. Single-roll dissolves are just as commonplace although, in my opinion, not as good for 16 mm film as optical dissolves printed directly from A and B rolls. As you cannot overlap two pieces of film on a single roll it is obvious that the effect must be produced on a single strip of film if it is to be cut into one reel of edited negative, so, if you want dissolves in a single-roll negative, you must make a duplicate in which the two actions are visually overlapped. To do this you first of all mark up your editing print in wax pencil in the way described above. You then look at the edge numbers alongside the two shots of film you wish to merge together. When you have noted the numbers you should locate the original pieces of negative in the cans, which you have already carefully numbered. With great care cut these two shots out of the negative and splice them together, placing some protective spacing on each end. Remove the whole shots from the negative and not just the part which appears in your cuting copy.

Indicating single-roll opticals

When you have found the two pieces of original negative, send them to a laboratory with an optical order form. They will then produce the optical effect for you on a single piece of duplicate negative film. To do this they will use an optical printer, or they may simply produce a fine-grain print of the two pieces of negative you have supplied, and make them up into A and B rolls before reprinting them on duplicate negative stock. Optical order form books can be supplied by any laboratory. Optical orders are easy to complete. Just give details of the markings you have already drawn on your cutting copy. Specify the edge numbers at which you want the dissolve to begin and the points where you wish its centre and end to be. Also specify the point at which you want the duplicate negative which the laboratory will produce to start. You should always start a duplicate at the beginning of the shot even if the dissolve does not start until much later in it. If you simply duplicate the area where the optical occurs, there will be a visible difference in quality between the original and the dupe when you cut it in. If the whole scene is duped the difference will be less noticeable.

Using edge numbers

When you mark the beginning, middle and end of the dissolve or fade you may perhaps find that the point you wish to mark does not exactly coincide with a particular edge number. Perhaps one edge number covers several frames. How then do you specify the exact frame you want to point out? Here again there is a standard formula.

A foot of 16 mm film (40 frames). Edge numbers normally appear every 40 (or 20) frames. The head of the film is at the right (low-numbered) end, and the tail at the left (high-numbered) end.

Look for the nearest edge number and pick one frame on which a definite part of the number appears. Perhaps the number is JH3245974. That is a long number, and perhaps only the figures 74 are really clear enough to stand out without careful study. Write the whole number on your optical order form (or sheet as it is often called) and underline or mark a box round the figures 74. You have now pinpointed one specific frame. Now if you look again at the piece of film you will find that on either side of the edge number you have listed, there are two numbers nearby. One is JH3245973 and the other is JH3245975. From these you can gauge the film's direction. Now look again at the frame you have specified with a box. Where, in relation to that frame, is the start of the optical effect you require? Is it to the right or to the left? Is it nearer 3245973 or 3245975? Next of all count up the exact number of frames between the frame you have specified and the frame at which you want your effect to start, and write the number down. Now, note the direction. Is the start nearer the higher number than the one you first noted, or nearer that which is lower? If it is nearer the higher one you put a plus sign next to the number of frames you have just noted. If it is in the opposite direction, mark minus and you have then pinpointed the exact position where you want your optical to start. Follow the same procedure for the beginning, middle and end of your optical and you will be able to present the laboratory with detailed instructions.

When the laboratory have prepared a duplicate negative incorporating the optical effects you will be able to cut this single piece of film into your single reel of edited negative and the two pieces of the original can be filed away. As soon as they return your fades and dissolves, first of all check the material supplied to make sure it is exactly what you ordered. Check each frame to make sure the effect is what you want, and then cut the cutting copy made from the duplicate into your cutting copy.

Preparing titles

At about the same stage of editing as the ordering of opticals, you can start to prepare the main and end titles for the edited film. The amount of work involved will depend on the nature of the titles required. If the cameraman has simply shot title cards on which an artist has drawn a picture and the appropriate titles, all you will have to do is cut the shots into the cutting copy. You can jump them in with a cut, fade them in or out or dissolve from one title to another. A fade is smoother and perhaps more impressive, and at the end of the film it is always nicer to fade out rather than simply cut to black. If the cameraman was told how long each title needed to be he may have produced the fades for you. He may even have mixed from title to title. If he did not know exactly what was required, you will have to cue and order the necessary effects.

Superimposed titles

You may sometimes want to superimpose titles over a moving background. It is quite easy to do but it can be quite expensive, as there is reasonable amount of laboratory work involved, especially if the film you are cutting has been shot on negative. If it has been shot on reversal, the titles can be superimposed when copies are printed if you arrange for the master to be cut in A and B rolls and have the titles shot on a suitable high-contrast stock. If you want to superimpose titles over a background shot on negative film a duplicate negative will normally have to be made.

In either case you start by arranging for title cards to be made. They should consist of white lettering on a glossy black background. The glossy background is important, for it helps the laboratory to get the contrast necessary for superimposition. If the titles are drawn on matt black card it may be difficult to get a strong enough black, and light may pass through when the titles are superimposed and spoil the background. Now if the film you are cutting has been shot on reversal, the titles can be shot on black and white reversal stock which can be developed to maximum density to make the letters really stand out. You can then align the lettering in a synchronizer with the background material you want to use. Consider the lettering your A roll and the background your B roll. Edit them exactly to length and they can then be printed together to give a combined print of both lettering and background. For A and B roll masters this really presents no problem. You simply have the lettering on one roll and when it runs out you splice on opaque spacing. On the other roll you have the background, which carries through in the normal A and B roll manner up to the first optical effect, where the rolls are changed in the manner I have already described. If you want the lettering to appear coloured, ask the laboratory to tint it during printing. For reversal work I normally find white or yellow lettering is the most satisfactory. If you don't ask the labs to develop the lettering film to maximum density, or if you use matt card, which makes it difficult to attain a satisfactory contrast, when lettering and background are printed together light may be able to shine through the greyish black and fog the background and make the colour look washed out.

For similar reasons titles cannot be superimposed over negative in the manner I have just described. An intermediate duplicate must be produced. You will start in the same manner, with white lettering on glossy cards. Shoot the titles and process to maximum density. The laboratory can then make a *matte* to prevent the clear background on the negative (representing the black card area) fogging the background you want the titles superimposed on. You can indicate exactly where you want each title to start and how you want it to begin and end (cut, dissolve or fade?) by using the edge numbers of the background. You can also ask the laboratory to colour the lettering when they produce the dupe. Yellow or red titles can work well superimposed over 16 mm colour neg, and white is always acceptable, but much will, of course, depend on the background. Some laboratories make title dupes by using CRI stock. Others use the inter-positive and inter-negative processes: we shall be considering them both in the chapter dealing with the preparation of show prints. In either case you will receive a single optical negative with titles and background superimposed. All you have to do is cut the cutting print made from the dupe into your cutting copy.

Economical titles

Superimposed titles are not cheap to produce. The laboratory processes involved in negative work are costly, and in reversal work additional rolls have to be made up, so the costs of printing copies will be higher. They are, however, desirable if you want to give your film a professional polish. A cheaper alternative is to use title cards on their own. This, of course, is much simpler. You simply arrange for the cards to be shot on the same type of stock as the rest of your film. You can use coloured lettering and coloured backgrounds. There are hundreds of different styles of lettering to choose from. I don't find cards on their own are ever quite as effective as superimposed titles, but if money is short there is no reason why they should not be perfectly satisfactory.

Opticals on video

Nowadays many 16 mm productions are completed on video. Again it is a question of getting the best of both worlds and minimizing costs. Film titling and optical work is time-consuming and thus expensive. Even superimposing a simple roller caption over a moving background at the end of a programme can cost as much as ten or more 400 ft rolls of unexposed film. Complicated effects tend to be very costly and they can take a very long time to produce. I have already described the main processes involved. Even when you are superimposing a simple main title or freezing a frame it takes time to cut out the master film, indicate where the optical must occur and make all the intermediate positive or negative stages. It can take a week or more to get a simple job done and it will not be cheap. For those reasons many productions are now titled on video and complicated optical work is frequently added electronically. To do that you simply edit your film on 16 mm in the usual way and, instead of inserting duplicates for the opticals, make a note of where they are required and wait until editing is completed. You can then make a low-contrast telecine print of the final edited version without opticals or titles and take it and the final mix master soundtrack along to a video editing suite. The titles and any special effects you require can then be added electronically as the master film is dubbed on to a broadcast-quality videotape. That tape can be used for making subsequent video copies and your film print, without titles, can be filed away as an insurance policy in case the master videotape is ever accidentally wiped. If you need film copies this method of working will not do because the quality of the titles transferred again from tape to film (which you would need to do to make film copies) would not be good, but if you are only going to produce video copies it is the cheapest and most efficient way of doing the job. You can tint the titles, choose from a wide range of letterings, roll, flip or run the titles vertically or horizontally. In a matter of minutes you can insert fades and still frames, split-screen effects and so on. So that is another way in which 16 mm film and video can be used together to make the finished job cheaper without the economies looking obvious.

9

Master to show print

When your film has been dubbed and any opticals have been cut in, your work will be almost completed. You have got two main jobs left. The master magnetic soundtrack must be re-recorded so that comopt copies can be made, and the cutting copy must be matched to the master material. If the film is going to be recorded on video or televised you will not need comopt copies. so the first job I have just mentioned need not concern you.

Negative cutting

As I have already mentioned, the process of matching the uncut camera original (the master), be it negative or reversal, to your edited cutting copy is known as *negative cutting*. It is a specialist job and one editors do not normally do themselves, but to find out what is involved let us assume that on this occasion you are going to do the work yourself.

If you are going to neg-cut your own film this is the point at which you will appreciate why it is worth winding through your master material when it is first delivered from the laboratory and marking the appropriate edge numbers on the top of the cans. You now have to find a matching piece of either negative or colour master for every shot in your edited cutting copy. The first thing to do is to wind through the cutting copy on a flat rewind bench and make a list of the edge numbers of the shots you need. You can then turn from the cutting copy to the unedited negative or colour master. Find the lengths with the appropriate edge numbers and, with great care, cut them out and hang them in a spotlessly clean bin. You can now put the cutting copy on a film horse and in the first track of a synchronizer. If the synchronizer has integral soundheads make sure they are lowered before you start work or they will scratch the negative and ruin it completely. For negative cutting work it is best to use a synchronizer without any soundheads at all and to work in a room which is air-conditioned. Alongside your cutting copy, in the second track of the synchronizer, put a new leader or a length of spacing with a start mark level with the start mark on your cutting copy, and wind down to the first scene.

Look for the very first edge number and then find the matching piece of

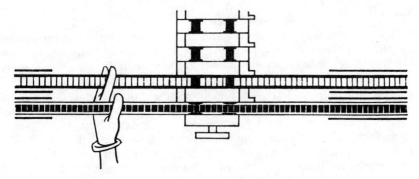

When negative cutting, the negative cutter runs the cutting copy in track one of the synchronizer, and matches the negative to it in track two.

master material. Place the number on the master material in the synchronizer exactly opposite the number on the cutting copy. Now run back to the start of the scene on the cutting copy and lightly mark the same point on the edge of the negative with a wax pencil. That point can now be cement-spliced to your new leader or spacing. Wind through to the end of the first shot and check the last edge number. Mark the point at which the shot ends and, allowing several frames for a splice to be made, cut the master material after the mark. Now you can repeat the action for the next shot. Find the appropriate piece of master material and match the edge numbers with those of the cutting copy. You will find it pays to double-check the numbers on either side. Run back to the start of the scene and mark it. That point can now be spliced to the end of the previous shot, and you can proceed in the same way until you have a complete reel of master which exactly matches your edited cutting copy.

You may sometimes find a scene which is too short to have an edge number on it. If that happens you will have to try to eye-match the action on the cutting copy with that on the master. It is not easy; that is why it is important when you are assembling your cutting copy to ensure that if there are any really short shots the edge numbers are noted and written on the cutting copy with a wax pencil. On optical duplicate material, you will also find you do not have edge numbers which match the cutting copy unless you have had a cutting print made from the dupe.

We have so far considered single rolls of master material. Let us now look at two alternative systems, one of which I have already briefly mentioned. The alternatives, which offer a number of advantages, are *checkerboards* and *A and B rolls*. We have already seen how, when master material is matched to an edited cutting copy, the appropriate numbers are matched and the scenes spliced together on a single roll. Thus the master matches the cutting copy in every detail. The method of working which I have described is exactly the same if you are matching a negative or a reversal master to the cutting copy. For A and B rolls there are slight differences in the procedure for negative materials and for reversal masters. To understand the differences, let us remind ourselves how the A and B system works.

A and B rolls

With the A and B system, the edited master (in the case of a reversal film) is matched to the cutting copy in exactly the same way as master material which is to be made up into a single roll. Only when the material is joined together does the difference between the A and B roll and the single roll become apparent. In the A and B system some shots are spliced, not to the next shot, but to black spacing. The picture moves from one roll to another whenever a fade or a dissolve is needed. The overlap required, if any, is carried through on the outgoing roll and brought in before the centre point of the effect on the incoming one. When the two rolls of master are printed on one positive roll, in the case of a dissolve, one scene is faded out and another faded in at the same point. The scene which is to be faded out is put on roll A, and the incoming scene is spliced on the opposite roll, or vice versa. The two lengths of film must be overlapped so that the laboratory can fade out roll A and simultaneously fade in roll B. The exact length of the overlap required depends on the length of the effect required. Half the optical length is needed, so if you want a 60-frame dissolve you will need 30 frames of overlap. On the outgoing roll, after the end of the overlap, and on the incoming roll before the overlap is started, you have to splice black spacing.

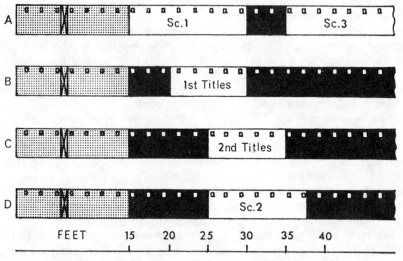

A and B assembly, with extra C and D rolls to allow titles to be superimposed and background shots to mix from scene one to scene two. Background of shot 1 on A mixes to background 2 on D at 27½ ft (note overlap). First title lettering cuts in on B at 20 ft and mixes to second on C at 27½ ft (again note overlap). The second title cuts out at 35 ft, and scene two on D mixes to scene 3 on A at 36 ft (again note overlap).

Now, when the two rolls are printed together on to a single roll of positive stock, the laboratory will make the necessary fade-out and fade-in. Both occur at the same point but they are printed from different rolls, so you end up with a dissolve.

Printing A and B opticals

You only need an overlap in the case of a dissolve or a wipe. In the normal course of events you join the end of the first shot to the start of the second on the same roll. For A and B roll printing you change from one roll to the other only when a dissolve or wipe occurs. In a dissolve or wipe you need to move from one scene to another gradually, and thus need to expose the two scenes together at the same point. As we have seen, you need an overlap to make this possible.

When you are fading in or fading out, however, you will not need any overlap, for you are only concerned with the exposure of one scene at a time. Thus it is unnecessary to move from one roll to the other.

Make a note of the footages of all optical effects and send a cue sheet to the laboratory when you order your prints. Tell them the footage and the effects and what is on each roll. For example, if you want a fade-out at 516 ft, tell them which roll the outgoing and incoming scenes are on and how long, in frames, you want the fade-out and fade-in to be.

What is the advantage of this A and B system? The main benefit is that you are printing from the original material, not from a single piece of duplicate film which has been produced simply to incorporate the optical effect. As the original is being used, prints will be of better quality.

On the start of each roll of A and B roll assembly you must mark a start point and the roll number and film title. State which is roll A and which is roll B and, if the first scene starts on roll A, build up B with black spacing. If you have a main title at the beginning which has to be superimposed over a moving background, in the A and B assembly you simply cut the background on one roll and the lettering on the other, building up the parts where there is no lettering with black spacing. When you come to the first optical, move from one roll to the other, where it can be joined scene to scene. Carry on until you reach the next optical, where the materials can again be transferred from one roll to the other, overlapping if a dissolve is required.

Sometimes, perhaps, you may want to carry a title through a dissolve. In this case you place your dissolve on the A and B rolls in the normal manner, and make up an extra C roll for the lettering. Mark a suitable start mark on the head of roll C level with the starts for the other two rolls. Build up the track where not in use with spacing in the normal manner. There is no limit to the number of rolls you can add.

I have said that the roll not in use must be built up with black spacing. It is a good idea to do this right through an A and B roll assembly, but it is essential at points where titles are to be superimposed and scenes are to dissolve. If you think for a moment of the processes involved, the reason will become obvious. You are dealing with two simultaneous exposures. If you expose two scenes on top of each other, you must take care to see that you get only the effect you want.

If you splice white or clear spacing on to the end of the lettering you hope to superimpose, the printer light will flood through the clear film and fog the picture you are simultaneously exposing from another roll. If you have black spacing, it will stop unwanted light passing through the printer. Only the lettering, which must always be on a really black background, will

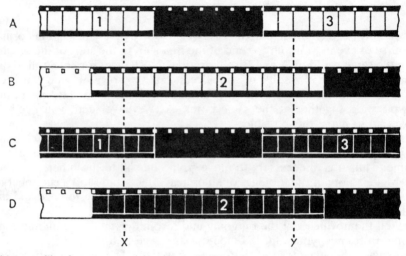

Title assembly of master material, using A, B, C and D rolls and allowing for a title to be superimposed over a moving background. Backgrounds and letterings mix from one to the other. A1, Background of first title. B2, Background of second title. A3, Background of third title. C1, Lettering of first title. D2, Lettering of second title. C3, Lettering of third title. X and Y are centres of dissolves (note the overlap).

shine through. Thus the background remains clear and correctly exposed. This is, of course, only true in the case of reversal masters.

When working with negative film you have a problem. If you want to superimpose titles you may find it best to make a duplicate negative incorporating the superimposition. This is because when you shoot white lettering on a black background on negative film the negative, when processed, will show black letters on clear film. On negative, you will remember, the tones of the original scene are reversed. If you print this on top of another scene the clear background will fog the other piece of film when it is exposed on top of it. So you must take precautionary measures. Make a fine-grain print of the background and shoot the titles on negative film. Make a high-contrast print of the titles and ask the laboratory to superimpose the high-contrast print and the fine-grain print and so make a negative that you can use for printing. This applies to superimposing negative titles. Most A and B roll printing methods can be applied equally well to negative or reversal, and A and B opticals are just as good as those on reversal film and equally easy to achieve. To get the best of all possible worlds, if the film you are cutting has been shot on 16 mm colour neg and titles need to be superimposed have the titles and backgrounds duped with the titles suitably matted by the laboratory. Cut the new dupes with the shots making up the rest of the film into A and B rolls or checkerboard.

Checkerboarding

There is one alternative to A and B printing – a system known as checkerboarding. It is basically the same as A and B, but instead of changing from one roll to the other only at opticals, the change is made at the end of each shot. If shot one starts on roll A, shot two will be on roll B. At the end of shot one black spacing is joined on roll A and the same spacing precedes shot two on roll B. This is carried through to the end of the film, putting each shot on a different roll and building up the blank spaces with black spacing. The small white flash which can betray 16 mm negative splices will not appear. The checkerboard system eliminates it.

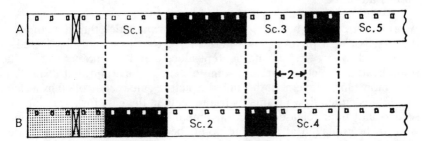

Checkerboard assembly. Both rolls start with leaders of equal length and with level start marks. Scene 1 is on roll A, roll B simultaneously containing blank spacing. Scene 2 is on B – a straight cut from 1 on A. Scene 3 is on A – a level cut from 2 on B. Scene B on A dissolves to scene 4 on D (note the overlap). Scene 5 is a straight cut on roll A. In a checkerboard assembly, each alternate shot is on a different roll.

When you splice negative always use fresh cement and a really clean splicer. Make sure that the sync bench is dust-free and do not use bent reels. You should always wear white linen gloves when you are handling negative and it is wise to mark only the edges of the film with your wax pencil. When you have finally matched all the scenes of your cutting copy to the master material, you will have either a complete cut negative or a cut colour master from which further prints can be produced. But before you can make the final show print you must choose the kind of soundtrack you want it to have.

Types of show prints

There are two main kinds of print for general showing. One has an optical, photographic soundtrack; the other has one which is recorded on a magnetic stripe on the edge of the print. On 16 mm the quality of magnetic recordings usually exceeds that of an optical track, but, unfortunately, many projectors are unable to project magnetically striped prints, so optical tracks are much more common. Many 16 mm productions are also shown on video. Let us look at the different systems.

16 mm prints with magnetically striped soundtracks are easy to record but quite difficult to check. The sound is recorded on a stripe of brown ferrous oxide coating on the side of the print: your final mix master recording made in the dubbing theatre can be re-recorded on to a magnetically striped print. Simply send the track with the print to a suitable transfer studio and ask them to transfer the master recording to the striped print. That will not alter the recording on the master in any way. It will

simply reproduce it on the striped print. Before the sound is transferred you must be sure that it is in correct synchronization with the action. Up to now in the cutting room you have been working in level sync, with sound and picture directly opposite each other, but when copies for projection are made that situation has to be changed. To understand why there has to be a change think about the layout of a sound film projector.

Sound advance

A projector consists basically of a feed reel from which the film comes in the first place, a picture gate where the picture is actually projected, a soundhead where the sound is reproduced and a take-up reel. The soundhead and picture gate are some distance apart, and that distance is very important. Movement through the picture gate is controlled by a claw. The film is pulled down frame by frame, held in the gate for a fraction of a second and then released. The movement is intermittent. Now if sound were to be replayed at the same point, because of the jerkiness of that movement the quality would be unusable: it would wow and be very distorted. So the soundheads on a projector are set well away from the disturbance. The distance between the picture gate and the soundhead is known as the *sound advance*. On a 16 mm film the sound is exactly 26 frames ahead in the case of an optical soundtrack, and 28 frames in the case of a magnetically striped one. So, when your master recording is transferred to a striped print ready for projection the sound must be advanced by 28 frames. The sound studio will advance the gate mark on the soundtrack by 28 frames before transferring the soundtrack on to the striped print. When the print is projected sound will be on the soundhead at the same time as the appropriate picture is in the picture gate 28 frames away; perfect synchronization is thus assured.

Magnetically striped prints are usually very good quality. If you want a striped copy you can ask the laboratory to print the master on pre-striped stock or you can have a stripe put on a copy after it has been printed. Don't stripe prints which are full of splices. The joins will be uneven, and it will be difficult to coat the surface of the film with an even stripe. It is always far better to make a new print, free from joins. That is particularly important to the solitary worker who likes to shoot his own film and edit the master material direct. He then sends his edited master away to be striped and records on the stripe. He would do far better to make a cutting print from his uncut master. He can then edit that and, when it is ready, match the master to it. From the matched master he can produce a new, clean print without splices. If that is striped, he will achieve far better results than if he stripes his cutting copy. The big drawback with magnetically striped prints is that there are very few projectors (outside professional preview theatres) which are equipped to show them.

Optical tracks

The alternative system is the optical soundtrack. It is far more widely used because there are many more outlets for combined optical prints and because it is an older system and people are used to it. It is also much easier to check an optical soundtrack–the modulations are visible and faults can often be seen by those experienced enough to know what to look for. The quality of optical sound is nowhere near as good as magnetic recordings but in some situations you may find you have to have a comopt print to get your film shown. The introduction of videocassettes (which have reasonably good quality magnetic sound) has opened up many new outlets, but 16 mm films with optical soundtracks are likely to be around for a good many years to come.

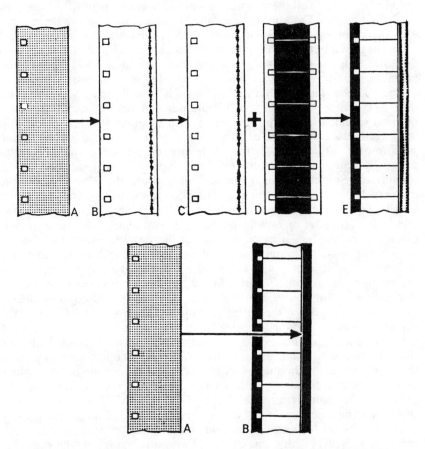

Stages of making a combined optical sound print (*above*). The master magnetic (A) is re-recorded on optical sound negative (B), which is then printed together with the picture negative (C and D) on positive stock to make a combined print (E). Stages of making a striped sound print (*below*). Re-record (transfer) master magnetic (A) to striped print (B).

As I mentioned earlier, optical soundtracks are produced by a photographic process. An optical track has to be printed and developed in the normal manner. A negative must first be produced and it can be made from your final mix master magnetic recording. How do you arrange for this negative to be made, and prepare it and the picture for printing?

Synchronizing optical sound for printing

Before you do anything else, mark an audibly recognizable point on the master magnetic recording. The accepted way to do this is to replace one frame of the leader with a frame of 1000-cycle tone which, when played, will reproduce as a 'plop' or 'bleep'. Note exactly where you put this sync tone, then send your magnetic track away for sound transfer. Ask the transfer suite to transfer it to optical sound negative, making sure you tell them the gauge of the track required: 16 mm for 16 mm printing and 35 mm for 35 mm prints. Tell them, too, the kind of negative you will be using to print the picture. The kind of track they produce must be the same type, with the emulsion in the same position. Ask them to produce an optical sound negative but, if you are going to make married (combined) prints, do not ask for a print of the soundtrack alone. They will transfer the magnetic sound to optical negative and develop it and return it to you.

You are now faced with a reel of squiggly modulations. Somehow you have to synchronize it with your picture negative before you can produce married sound prints of picture and sound together. At this point, you must again place the edited negative or colour master in the film horse and synchronizer. Again make sure there are no magnetic soundheads to physically damage the picture or track. Now take a good look at the soundtrack. Somewhere near the beginning you will find that plop – the frame of 1000-cycle tone which you attached to the leader. It will be quite easy to find – one frame of closely spaced lines which are bigger in the middle than they are on either side. Now, do you remember where you put this frame on the leader of the magnetic? Place the recorded plop on the negative opposite that same point on the picture leader. Your sound is now in level synchronization with the picture, exactly like the magnetic track recorded in the dubbing theatre. So far so good; but remember you are now synchronizing an optical track which is going to be used to produce a combined print. When that print is projected on a sound projector, the sound will need to be farther ahead than the picture–26 frames ahead in the case of a 16 mm married optical print. You must, therefore, advance the plop on the optical sound negative by 26 frames and then replace it in the synchronizer. It should now occur 26 frames before the point at which you attached a frame of tone to the leader of the master magnetic recording–26 frames nearer the head of the roll. When you are satisfied that this is the case, wind back to the very beginning of the reel and splice some spacing on to both picture and sound negative. Mark a large start mark on both level with each other, and write in clear letters the words '16 mm print, sync. Start'. You should then wind down in sync to the end of the roll and put another sync mark there, identifying it as '16 mm print sync. End'.

You may think it is unnecessary to mark sync at both the beginning and end of the negative, but it is a good idea to do so. It gives you a double check if things go wrong, and there are a few laboratories which print the picture from the beginning of the roll to the end and then print the track in the opposite direction. It is also essential to mark the exact nature of the sound separation on both sound and picture near the appropriate start marks. If a start mark alone is put on without explanation, someone may well assume the two pieces of film are supplied in level synchronization and pull up the sound a further 26 frames.

For 35 mm printing the procedure is almost exactly the same. Only the distance of the separation differs. On a 35 mm comopt print the sound is advanced 20 frames. That does not, of course, apply when 35 mm pictures are reduction-printed with a 16 mm soundtrack. As the reduction print is going to be shown on a 16 mm projector, the advance must be 26 frames. The projector which will show the finished product dictates the sound advance required, and for 16 mm prints with optical soundtracks, 26 frames is internationally standard.

Ordering prints

Now you can order your first print. It is always a good idea to ask the laboratory to clean the material they will use to make the print. Tell them too what you are sending. They will want to know if it is negative or reversal. They should be told if it is in level sync or printing sync, and colour or black and white. Again, tell them exactly what you require. How many prints, and what kind of prints are you in need of?

If you are ordering the first print of a new film do not expect results overnight, particularly if it is in colour. All new films have to be carefully graded. Each light change must be worked out to ensure that every scene matches the one which precedes it. A detailed shot list can be helpful, particularly where the film contains night scenes. Sometimes the cutting copy can also be useful if there are a number of complicated opticals.

As I have already mentioned earlier in this book, the various film formats are interchangeable: 16 mm productions can be copied on 35 mm film and vice versa. Your 16 mm film can also be shown on video. Nowadays it is very likely that you will need to know how to make copies on videocassette, so let us spend a few minutes considering what you will need to do to produce copies in the various formats. Let's take enlarging first.

You have edited a film which is so good the producer wants to get it shown on the cinema circuits. The film has been shot on 16 mm colour negative. You have edited a 16 mm cutting copy and the original negative has been matched to it and you have had your first graded colour print, which has delighted everyone. Now the producer needs a 35 mm copy. What must you do?

Blowing up 16 mm to 35 mm

First you must ensure that the laboratory you are dealing with has the equipment and the experience needed to handle blow-up work. Not every 16 mm laboratory wants to do so and you may find you have to look around. Large companies like Technicolor and Rank have got the business down to a fine art. If you only want one 35 mm copy you can enlarge the 16 mm original negative by printing it directly on to 35 mm colour positive stock using an optical printer. That will work well for one copy, but if you need more than one copy you will not want to risk the wear and tear involved in repeatedly handling the original negative. You will need a duplicate. If you are expecting to make a number of 35 mm copies that duplicate should be a 35 mm one. Ask the laboratory to blow up your 16 mm cut neg to a 35 mm *colour reversal internegative*, usually simply referred to as a *CRI*. The cost of 35 mm copies will then be reduced because they can be made by contact printing the new 35 mm internegative on 35 mm positive stock, which will be cheaper than making a blow-up print every time.

A 16 mm colour negative original can be enlarged in two different ways. It can be directly blown up to a 35 mm colour reversal internegative using an optical printer. Alternatively, a 16 mm *colour interpositive* can be contact-printed from the 16 mm original cut neg. That interpositive can then be optically printed on a roll of 35 mm internegative stock. Whichever way you work, if the original is good quality you should not have any problems. Because the reversal internegative is reached in one stage the quality should be better than going via an intermediate colour interpositive, but nowadays, with fine-grain film stocks, the difference will not be great. Before you enlarge anything to 35 mm make sure the original is good. If it is not, do not waste your money. As you enlarge the picture any imperfections will be magnified: if you have soft focus, scratches or other problems on your 16 mm cut neg you will simply be throwing your money away.

Enlarging 16 mm colour reversal

If the film you are cutting has been shot on 16 mm colour reversal, making a 35 mm blow-up is just as straightforward. Send the cut master to your laboratory and ask them to make a 35 mm *colour blow-up internegative*. They will then re-expose the cut 16 mm colour master on 35 mm colour negative stock and produce 35 mm colour prints by printing on to 35 mm colour positive. The quality of copies produced in this way can be extremely good if the original was shot on a low-contrast stock like Ektachrome.

Black and white blow-ups

Films shot on 16 mm in black and white can be enlarged to 35 mm in much the same way, though the terminology used is different. There are no internegatives in black and white. They are simply known as *dupe (duplicate) negatives*. There are no reversal internegatives either. So, if you want a 35 mm copy of a film shot on 16 mm black and white negative, you an either enlarge the 16 mm cut neg by printing it optically on to 35 mm positive stock, or you can contact-print the 16 mm neg on a 16 mm *fine-grain duping positive*, which is a low-contrast intermediate stage. That fine-grain dupe pos can then be optically printed on 35 mm negative, which can be contact-printed on 35 mm positive stock to produce copies in the usual way. If the film has been shot on 16 mm black and white reversal you simply optically print (blow-up) the 16 mm cut master on to 35 mm dupe negative.

16 mm black and white from colour

A 16 mm colour original can also be used to make 16 mm black and white copies. You may recall that I mentioned this possibility when we were considering rush prints. Monochrome prints are cheaper than colour ones and if a vast footage has been shot and economies need to be made, printing a black and white cutting copy will help. The colour original can be printed directly on to black and white positive stock. 16 mm originals can also be reduced to 8 mm.

Reduction printing

It is just as easy to make 16 mm copies of 35 mm originals. 35 mm feature films are reduced to 16 mm for showing on ships, schools, prisons and a number of other special locations. Copies are made by *reduction printing*. Films shot on 35 mm negative can be reduction-printed straight on to 16 mm positive stock, but that method is not recommended if several copies are required. If a number of prints are needed it is better to make a 16 mm *reduction dupe negative*, from which copies can be produced by contact printing.

16 mm copies from 35 mm B/W negatives

If you want 16 mm copies of a film shot on 35 mm black and white negative you can get them by contact-printing the 35 mm cut negative on 35 mm fine-grain positive stock. That copy, known as a fine-grain duping positive, can then be reduction-printed on to 16 mm negative. Process the negative and print it on 16 mm positive stock.

16 mm copies from 35 mm colour negatives

If the 35 mm original is in colour you can make 16 mm copies in three different ways. If you only want one copy the cost of making a duplicate negative may not be justified, so you can simply print the 35 mm original cut negative on 16 mm colour positive stock via a reduction printer. If you want several copies there are two alternative courses you can take. The best way to do the job is to make a 16 mm reduction colour reversal internegative (CRI). You can make a CRI in one stage without any intermediate positive, so the quality should be good. Ask the laboratory to reduction-print the original cut 35 mm colour negative on to 16 mm CRI stock, process the internegative and print it with a re-recorded optical track: you will get first-class-quality copies. The alternative way of going about it is to ask the laboratory to print the 35 mm colour neg on 35 mm colour interpositive stock–the colour equivalent of the fine-grain duping pos used in black and white work. When the interpos has been processed it

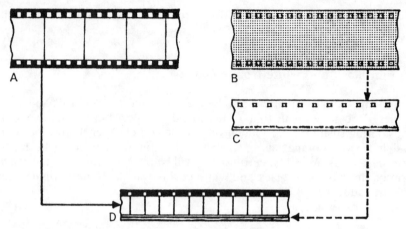

16 mm married direct reduction prints from 35 mm negative. The 35 mm negative (A) is reduction printed with a re-recorded 16 mm optical sound negative (C) on 16 mm positive stock (D). The 16 mm optical sound negative is made by re-recording from the 35 mm master magnetic (B).

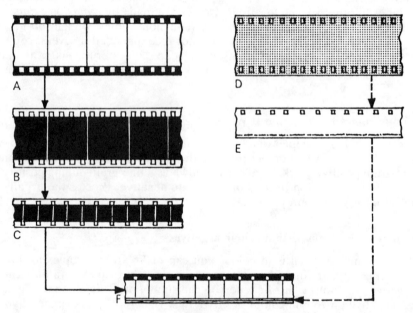

Making a number of 16 mm married prints from a 35 mm black-and-white negative. The 35 mm negative (A) is printed on 35 mm fine grain positive (B) which is itself printed on to 16 mm reduction dupe negative (C). The 35 mm master magnetic (D) is simulaneously re-recorded on 16 mm optical sound negative (E). The two 16 mm negatives (C) and (E) are then printed together on 16 mm positive stock (F).

can be reduction-printed on to 16 mm colour internegative stock. Process the interneg and you are in business. You can print it on 16 mm colour stock and make all the copies you need.

Enlarging and reducing sound

We have so far discussed various ways of enlarging and reducing pictures shot in the various film formats. We have not yet discussed sound, but you may find you need to end up with comopt prints at the end of the blow-up or reduction process. If you are blowing up a 16 mm film for cinema release you are certain to have to produce 35 mm comopt prints. It is equally possible that if you are reducing a 35 mm film to 16 mm you will need 16 mm comopt prints at the end of the day, so let's see how you can produce them.

When you have finished dubbing you will have a 16 mm master final mix magnetic soundtrack. If your film hs been shot on 16 mm colour neg and you have to make 35 mm comopt colour prints you can enlarge the picture by following the steps we have just explored, but what about the soundtrack? You cannot print from a 16 mm mag track and you cannot enlarge a 16 mm optical soundtrack. To get the optimum possible quality all you need to do is to arrange for your 16 mm final mix master magnetic track to be re-recorded as a 35 mm optical sound negative. Get the negative developed but don't print it until it has been synchronized to the new 35 mm internegative (or dupe neg if the film is in black and white). The sound will need to be advanced by 20 frames, so when prints are projected on a 35 mm projector sound and picture are in perfect synchronism.

If you are reducing a 35 mm original to 16 mm and want to make 16 mm comopt prints you will also need to re-record the soundtrack. If a 35 mm optical sound neg exists it is technically possible to reduce it to 16 mm using a reduction printer but the quality is not good. It is much better to make a completely new recording. So, if you have a film shot on 35 mm colour negative and a 35 mm master final mix magnetic soundtrack and want to make 16 mm comopt colour copies, you will need to make either a reduction *reversal* internegative or a 35 mm interpositive and then a 16 mm reduction *internegative* for the picture, and re-record the 35 mm final mix mag as a 16 mm optical sound negative. Make sure you get the geometry right, with the emulsion in the correct position for printing with the picture dupe. As you are going to be making 16 mm comopt copies, when you put the new internegative and sound negatives in sync for printing you will need to advance the sound by 26 frames.

Making video copies

All the film formats can be satisfactorily copied on video. You are almost certain to have to deal with video copying at some stage of your work in the cutting room, so let's consider that procedure. Remember the fundamental difference between the two media, film and video. It can be summed up in two words. Film is a *photographic* process. Video is *electronic*. When a film cameraman shoots a scene with a film camera the stock he uses records the image on a photographic emulsion, which is then processed. When a video cameraman shoots the same scene the image he films is converted to a series of electronic signals which are recorded on videotape. Hold a processed film up to the light and you can immediately see the image it records. Hold a videotape up in the same way and you will see (and hear) nothing, for without suitable equipment it cannot be replayed. So, how can you bring the two fundamentally different media together and make video copies of your finished film?

The first point to remember is that video does not like extreme contrasts of lighting. If you try to record a very contrasty colour film on videotape it may not look very good. If you record one which is low-contrast it will look much better, so always try to start with a master which the electronic equipment is going to be able to cope with satisfactorily. If you have a 16 mm film shot on colour negative, the original negative can be recorded directly on to videotape with the image *reverse-phased* as it runs through. You start with your film negative, in which the tones of the original scene are reversed, and end up with a videotape copy, in which they are as they were when the scene was filmed. The laboratory or specialist video facilities house will lace up your 16 mm neg on a telecine machine and lock it electronically to a video recorder. As the negative is transferred to tape at normal projection speed it can be colour-graded (timed). This method of transferring negative to video produces excellent quality results. Many major TV series are now produced working this way. Indeed there are some who feel that shooting on colour film, developing the original neg and recording it directly on to videotape gives a sharper image and better overall quality than shooting on video in the first place. It is equally easy to shoot on 16 mm colour reversal and re-record the master on video via a telecine. Again, if the original is low-contrast, the results should be fine.

Electronic film conforming

When the method I have just described of putting film on video is used, the tape resulting from the transfer can be edited in a number of different ways. It can be done entirely on tape by a video editor in a video edit suite. He can work either on- or off-line. If he works *on-line* he will work with the broadcast-quality master tape resulting from the telecine transfer throughout. If he works *off-line* he will edit a low-band copy with a time code. When the final shape of the programme has been determined the master tape will be electronically matched by a computer to the edit made on the off-line copy. Using a process known as *Electronic Film Conforming (EFC)*, which is now operated by a number of specialist laboratories, it is equally possible for the programme to be cut on film. When the master film has been processed a 16 mm cutting copy is printed in the normal manner. The master is then recorded on videotape. You cut the cutting copy and use it for all the various editing processes just as you do when editing any film, but when you have completed the job, instead of sending your edited work print to a negative cutter to have the master matched to it, you have the videotape conformed to match it electronically, using EFC technology. The laboratory will note the cuts you have made by logging the edge number on your cutting copy. Those numbers are then fed into a computer, which makes the same edits on tape, producing a video edit master incorporating all the necessary optical effects. Titles can be added at this stage. Finally your 16 mm final mix master magnetic soundtrack is recorded on the video edit master ready for video release copies to be made.

The EFC process is not widely used, but it is becoming more and more popular as those who have tried it tend to use it again and again. It is not suitable or cost-effective for every job, but the quality is good because final show copies are produced with the minimum number of intermediate stages. If you have to prepare different versions of your film and only need video copies, the EFC process is ideal, for you can make as many different versions as you wish without actually cutting the original. I recently edited a series of films about a major property development in the centre of London. The films were shot over a three-year period, and various versions were released as the work progressed. The material was shot on 16 mm colour negative. The neg was processed and recorded on videotape. I then cut a 16 mm cutting copy. When the first film was completed, six months after work on site began, the video master was electronically conformed to match my 16 mm edited cutting copy and video copies were run off. The original remained uncut, so when the building company wanted a different version of the same story six months later, I simply recut my cutting copy and the video was again matched to it to produce the new version. If I had worked on film throughout, when the first version was completed the original 16 mm negative would have had to be cut to make 16 mm prints: to make a second production using the same material would have meant making expensive colour internegatives of everything before cutting could begin. Working with video we had excellent quality through-out, and all the original material to work with.

Cutting video productions on 16 mm film

The same EFC process can also be used to edit programmes shot on video on 16 mm film. Instead of making a video copy for on- or off-line editing the video master can be telerecorded on film. The *telerecording* (also known as a *Kinescope*) can then be edited in the normal way. When you have finished your work the master tape can be conformed to match your telerecorded cutting copy and your 16 mm final mix master soundtrack can be dubbed alongside. This method of working is really only worth adopting when there is not a very high footage of original material involved. If there is, the cost of making and processing a telerecorded cutting copy will be higher than making an off-line video copy, and there may be little or no cost advantage. If film cutting equipment is available and video is not, working in the way I have just described will enable you to get first-class professional results with a video master programme using the equipment in your film cutting room, but make sure your laboratory is equipped to handle EFC work before you start work. If you have problems, Filmatic Laboratories in London, who have done much to pioneer the wider use of EFC technology, may well be able to help you. If you want to get the best of both worlds you can make a low band video copy with burned-in time code of the master videotape and edit it off line to make a first assembly. You can then telerecord that assembly on 16 mm film from the low band cassette and fine cut the telerecording. Lay tracks to match the 16 mm copy and dub it in the usual way. The original master tape can then be matched to your fine cut 16 mm print by using EFC techniques and the time code and the master final mix magnetic track can be recorded alongside. You can thus enjoy all the advantages of fine cutting and dubbing on film and the cost saving of not printing thousands of feet of film rushes.

Putting film on videotape

Electronic techniques, with help from film, are now used in one way or another in the production of many major TV series, but there are still many producers and editors who prefer to work on film until editing has been completed. Programmes are shot on film and cut and dubbed using 16 mm equipment. When the programme has been finalized and the master matched to the edited cutting copy, a low-contrast telecine show print is produced and recorded with the final mix master magnetic on video. For optimum quality the cut neg can be put on tape instead of a low-contrast telecine print, but if the master has been neg cut in A and B rolls you will find that many telecine facilities houses are unable to handle it and will prefer to work from a single-roll print. A video copy made directly from an original negative or colour master will usually look better than one made from a show print, but in the hands of a competent laboratory a well-graded show print will look very good and the average television viewer is unlikely to notice the difference. So, if you have to make video copies of your 16 mm film you can either arrange for the cut neg to be graded and put straight on to tape with your final mix master soundtrack, or you can ask the lab to make a low-contrast telecine print and use that.

Working either way you will be able to run off as many copies as you wish. If you are planning to make a number of tape copies it is worth making a duplicate master on one-inch or any other broadcast-quality tape. If you do not do that, the film will have to be laced up on a telecine machine every time a video copy is required, and that will be expensive. It will be cheaper and more efficient to make a video master from your final show print and use that for duplicating bulk copies.

Checking film prints

When the laboratory delivers your first graded print you will sit down and look at it with a critical eye. It is a very pleasant feeling seeing the first show print of a film you have cut. If you have been cutting in black and white and the film was shot in colour this will be the first time you have seen a colour copy. You may be looking at the result of days or months of your work, but your job is still not quite finished. You will need to ensure that the show prints, and any internegatives or dupes made to produce bulk copies, are up to standard. The first graded copy is sometimes known as an *answer print* or a *check print*. When you sit down and look at it what should you look for? There are a number of points to check. Is it scratched? Is it in sync? Those are just two of a number of questions you must ask yourself. Are any of the shots too light or too dark and do the colours look right from scene to scene? Are there any neg cutting errors?

Scratches are amongst the most common faults on both prints and negatives. Generally speaking, print scratches are black, though this can also apply to some scratches on negative, particularly those which have been caused in the camera. If you suspect your print is scratched, stop the projector and have a look at the print under a light. You can usually see a scratch if it is on the print itself. If it is on the cellulose side you may be able to get it polished or waxed out, but if it is on the emulsion side there is little you can do unless you are checking a new print, when you can, of course, send it straight back to the laboratory. On library material it is quite possible that a scratch may be in the original material. Nothing you can do to your copy will improve it. The same applies to duplicate negatives and negatives made from colour masters and reversal materials. If the scratch is not on the print you are looking at, you will have to check back each stage until you find it, if you wish to remedy the fault.

Negative scratches often appear white on the screen. The exceptions to this are, as I have mentioned, some camera scratches, which may appear black. If the scratch has occurred before the original material was developed you can often find a small kink in the scratch at either the top or the bottom. Alas, little can be done to remedy this kind of fault.

Other faults common on new prints are dirt and sparkle. Dirt on a print is usually black, and dirt on a negative prints as white sparkle. Dirt on the print itself can be cleaned off with a clean antistatic cloth immersed in carbon tetrachloride, but negative dirt must be removed before a print is made.

When you have checked your first print you are left with just two jobs. You must clear up the cutting-room and make a note of the copyright materials you have used in your final edited version. Let us consider copyright first.

Clearing copyright

As we have seen in an earlier chapter, royalty payments for library material, and the use of copyright recordings of music and sound effects, are assessed on the amount of material used in the final edited version, and also on the type of distribution the finished film is to have. Normally a fixed sum is charged for each thirty seconds of sound used from any particular recording. A film library will also charge a set fee per foot of film used in the final edited version. The exact charge will depend on the kind of audience the finished film is to be shown to. Thirty seconds of music or a few feet of library material used in a specialist training film which is only going to be shown to audiences of American doctors will cost much less than the same material used in an advertising commercial destined for worldwide television showing. When the film is finished, run through the final soundtrack and note the footage at which each piece of library film or commercial recording starts and ends and calculate the overall length you have used. Send the facts, possibly with a copy of the dubbing cue sheet, to the film production office, who will arrange for it to be relayed to the appropriate licensing authority.

Clearing up the cutting room

With this last editing task done, you can turn to tidying up the cutting room. What a reward for a few months' work! How untidy have you let it become and what are you to do with the materials you are left with? When you have seen an answer print or a show print you are happy with, the trims of your cutting copy can be thrown away. The soundtracks you mixed together in the dubbing theatre can be reclaimed, but be sure you do not accidentally reclaim any of your new master recordings. You can reclaim the spacing from your dubbing tracks and join it up into rolls ready for use on a future production. Throw away short lengths of magnetic track unless you want to keep the sound effects and build up your own sound effects library. If you have a number of long lengths of reclaim sound you can join them together and use them again. Lengths shorter than 100 ft are probably not worth keeping. If you can make up a reclaim roll of 1000 ft with only a few joins it may be suitable for use in recording effects for future productions, but if there are going to be a lot of joins it is not worth keeping. It probably is worth keeping the trims of your colour master or cut negative. If the subject is of general interest you may be able to sell it to a library for use as stock shots. I stress that the material must be of general interest. Shots of the works foreman having tea, which the cameraman enjoyed shooting but which you never used, will not be welcomed by a library either!

Film storage

Before you leave the cutting room for the last time you should carefully label and store all your master materials. Keep the master final mix and M and E tracks and the cut picture master. It is also worth keeping the cutting copy and the cue sheets in case you want to dub a foreign-language version. Label them carefully with the name of the production company and its address on top so that the cans need never be lost. Write the full film title and the exact nature of the material on the label. It is useless just writing 'MAG' on your master track. Someone might think it is blank and use it again, and then you will be in trouble. State exactly what the material is. If it is a master track say so, and then say exactly what kind of master it is. A detailed label should tell you everything. 'OPERATION MAGIC CARPET–MASTER MAG' is inadequate. 'OPERATION MAGIC CARPET, 16 MM FINAL MIX MASTER. ENGLISH VERSION. CENTRE TRACK. ROLL 1 OF 1' is much more useful. If you are going to keep the cans in racks, the material in them will be easier to find if you first of all side-label them. Always keep film at a reasonable temperature. Avoid extremes of heat and cold and, above all, damp. From time to time it pays to wind each roll through and check its condition. If you take simple precautions the film you have edited should last a lifetime.

  You may perhaps think that labelling cans is such a simple job nothing could ever go wrong. If you do, I know one assistant editor who would not agree with you. He had been working in the cutting rooms for about six months and had just assisted in the editing of two documentary films about dentistry. One of the films was aimed at audiences of dentists, the other was intended for showing to patients. They were both shot on 16 mm for release on video. When the productions were completed telecine graded show prints were made from the cut negative, and they and the final mix master soundtracks were kept in the cutting room waiting for the sponsor to order copies. Two weeks after the film were completed the assistant went off on holiday. While he was away the sponsor ordered a thousand video copies of the patients' version of the film, and a temporary assistant, who was standing in while the permanent assistant was on holiday, took the telecine print and master final mix out of the rack and sent them to be recorded on video. When the copies arrived the editor decided to look at one of them to check the quality. He took one of the thousand cassettes home, played it on his video recorder, and got a very unpleasant surprise. The picture showed the patients' version of the film, but the soundtrack was the one intended for audiences of dentists. The films were similar, so the error was not noticed when the copies were made, but from the sponsor's point of view the copies were useless, because the commentary made the wrong points to the wrong audience. Subsequent investigation showed how the error had occurred. The assistant who originally labelled the cans had simply written 'DENTAL FILM – FINAL MIX' on the labels and had failed to specify the versions. The temporary assistant was unaware that there were two versions, and in good faith sent off what he took to be the only master final mix. As a result a thousand video copies had to be re-recorded. So, attention to detail is important, even if you are only labelling cans.

As you gain more and more experience you will find that the job you have taken on becomes more and more enjoyable. There is something very satisfying about starting with a great pile of cans of scenes shot in no particular order and ending up with a thoroughly professional programme which audiences find interesting to watch. As with all jobs, you will find there are days when nothing seems to go right and you wish you were sitting safely in an office selling insurance, but as a film editor you will find those days, if they occur at all, are few and far between. There will inevitably be moments of crisis. You will find that, apart from mastering the basic techniques we have explored in this book, you will need additional qualities of patience and tact. You will get used to dealing with producers who think they know everything but actually know little or nothing about the medium they are using. You will probably also have moments of panic when your career seems to be coming to an abrupt end. I can recall many. There was the time when I was editing a key network TV talks programme transmitted every Monday to a very large audience. The Olympic Games were due to start the following day, and the programme we had cut was extremely topical and very tough in its approach to the subject. It had been shot over the weekend, and rushes had started to arrive in the cutting room late on the Sunday night. Transmission was scheduled for 8 o'clock on the Monday evening. We worked through the night and had the film ready for dubbing ninety minutes before transmission. It was a thirty-minute programme and we knew we were cutting it fine, but on that particular programme, which was always extremely topical, that was acknowledged to be part of the job. On that particular occasion, though we did not know it then, it was going to be an even tighter schedule than usual. As we took our seats in the dubbing theatre the producer introduced a man we had not seen before. 'This is the network solicitor,' he said calmly. 'As we are saying one or two controversial things in the course of the programme, the company feels he ought to see it before it goes out.'

'Fine,' we all said, aware that ninety minutes from then around fifteen million people would be tuning in their sets to watch a programme which had been well publicized in advance by the press, who knew it was going to be hot stuff. We never in our wildest dreams thought the solicitor would actually want to change anything, and assumed that if he saw anything he thought was doubtful he would simply arrange for the press officer to issue a disclaimer. How wrong we were. We sat there for an hour and five minutes as the programme was dubbed by an expert sound mixer used to working in a rush. We reached the end title music 25 minutes before air time. At first the solicitor said nothing; then, just as we were preparing to take the cutting copy, which was being used as a transmission print, up to telecine he turned to the producer and said, 'That scene where the javelin thrower accuses the selectors of accepting bribes will have to come out. There's no way we can let that pass.' The producer argued, as precious minutes slipped past, but the solicitor would not be swayed. 'That scene must be cut!'

With fifteen minutes to spare we ran up five flights of stairs to the cutting room. With the help of a pic sync we wound down and made the cut, putting in a cutaway which my excellent assistant had hung up in the right place in the bin. With five minutes to spare we ran down to telecine, which was in the basement. With two minutes left I thrust the reels of mag and picture into the hands of the telecine supervisor. He took them and ran to the telecine machine. As he started to lace up the film we could hear the presentation editor on talkback cueing telecine to stand by to roll after the next commercial. As the film was wound on to the take-up spool we heard the words 'Run telecine!' You cannot run it closer than that!

The experience I have just recalled, and others quite like it, are among the many things which make editing film more interesting than selling insurance. Chatting in a bar a few hours after that show was transmitted I was introduced to someone who asked what I did for a living. 'I'm a film editor,' I replied. 'Oh,' she said, 'You're the one who cuts out the bad bits.' If only she had seen what we had been doing a few hours earlier!

No doubt you will have similar experiences and I am sure that, once you have mastered the technicalities, you too will find film editing is fun.

I shall watch for your name on the end credits.

Glossary

Action When film is edited using separate soundtracks, the picture to which the tracks are matched is often called simply 'the Action'.

Big close-up (abbr. BCU) Shot taken very close to a subject, closer than would be necessary for a close-up—part of a human face, for example.

Blow-up The technique of producing a larger picture from a smaller-gauge film. 35 mm prints produced from 16 mm materials are known as blow-ups. 16 mm prints made from 8 mm are likewise blown up.

Clapper board (slate) Two pieces of board, hinged together in such a way that the two parts can be banged together at the start of a synchronized sound take. Scene and take number are written in chalk on the board so that the action can later be identified. The film editor matches the point where the two pieces of the board actually bang together with the corresponding bang on the sound track and is thus able to synchronize sound and picture.

Close-up (abbr. CU) Shot taken close to a subject and revealing detail. In the case of a human subject, a shot of the face only, the hands only, etc.

Colour master or original The name given to reversal colour materials exposed in the camera.

Combined print A print where soundtrack and action are printed together on the same piece of film stock. Also known as a **married print**.

Commentary Spoken words accompanying a film; the speaker usually remains unseen. Also **narration** or **off-screen narration and voice-over.**

Continuity The flow from one shot to another without breaks or discrepancies. Smoothness in the development of subject matter.

Contrast The difference between the lightest and the darkest parts of a shot.

Core A plastic centre on which film is sometimes wound.

Cross cut To alternate from one scene to another in the course of editing so that two or more subjects are presented in fragments, alternately.

Cue sheets (dubbing) When all separate soundtracks have been matched to the action of a cutting copy, the footage at which each sound starts and ends is marked on a cue sheet. This guides the sound mixer as he mixes tracks.

Cutaway A shot of something other than the main action. A cutaway is inserted between shots of the main action, often to bridge a time lapse or to avoid a **jump cut** (q.v.).

Cutting barrel See **Film bin.**

Cutting copy or work print Often abbreviated to simply **C/C**, the cutting copy is the name given to the print used for editing purposes.

Cutting room The film editor's kingdom. It contains all the equipment needed for editing sound and picture.

Dailies See **Rushes.**

Density Image blackness. A measure of the light transmitted by film.

Dissolve An optical effect in which one scene gradually replaces another. In essence a **fade-out** and a **fade-in** are superimposed. Also known as a **mix.**

Double system A system of sound recording used for shooting synchronized sound takes. Sound is recorded on separate magnetic film or tape and not (as in the single system) on the actual film in the camera.

Dubbing The name given to the various processes involved in re-recording a number of separate soundtracks to make one final mixed soundtrack. Also the name given to re-voicing a film in another language.

Dupe (Duplicate) A dupe neg is a duplicate negative, not the original exposed in the camera. It is usually produced by printing a suitable positive stock on unexposed negative material.

Duplicating Reversal materials, when printed on other reversal stocks, are often said to be duplicated. Where negative film is reproduced on positive stock the same process is known as printing.

Edge numbers Also known as **key numbers** and sometimes as **negative numbers**. On 16 mm film edge numbers are normally located on the edge of the film at intervals of either 20 frames or one foot (40 frames). The numbers originally occur on unexposed stock and are thus reproduced whenever the original material is printed. Used especially when the camera master (camera original) is matched to the edited cutting copy, and in the preparation of optical effects. Where edge numbers are missing or not legible, arbitrary numbers can be printed in ink on originals and prints. This is known as **coding** or **rubber-numbering.**

Editing machine In the USA the term 'Moviola', the trade name of a particular model, has now passed into general use to describe any editing machine.

Editing rack A bar with pins on which clips of film are hung

Editorial cut See **Level cut.**

Effects Sound effects. **FX** for short.

Emulsion The side of the film coated with light-sensitive materials (in the case of picture stock). The side of a magnetic track coated with ferrous oxide. Easily identified in either case as the less shiny of the two sides.

Fade-in Gradual emergency of a shot out of darkness.

Fade-out A shot that gradually disappears into complete darkness.

Film bin Large receptacle into which film is allowed to fall while assembling shots or when running film through a viewer or projector instead of using a take-up spool. In the USA **film barrel** or **cutting barrel** are the usual terms.

Final mix The final soundtrack, containing all music, dialogue, commentary and sound effects. This is the soundtrack the audience hears.

Fine-grain Film stocks with extremely fine-grain emulsions used for the intermediate stages in the course of producing duplicate materials.

Fine-grain positive, fine-grain master positive, or duplicating print Intermediate fine-grain or protection material sometimes indicated specifically by type, giving the number (e.g. EK-7255 or EK 7253).

Frame A single picture on a length of cinematograph film or the corresponding amount of a perforated magnetic soundtrack. The lines dividing a picture into frames horizontally are known as frame lines.

Grading or timing Estimating the amount of light that must be passed through individual scenes and the colour filtration required to obtain a perfect colour balance when producing prints or duplicate master materials. This operation relies to some extent on the experience of the technician concerned, who sometimes works with the help of a computerized Hazeltine Analyzer or Liner.

Inter-negative A duplicate colour negative. In the USA refers primarily to a colour negative derived directly from a colour reversal original, while other negatives are known as **colour dupe negatives**.

Inter-positive A fine-grain colour print used in the course of making duplicate colour negatives.

Jump cut A cut which breaks the continuity by omitting an interval of time, revealing persons or objects in a different position in two adjacent shots.

Laying sound To place sound in its correct relationship with picture.

Leader A blank piece of film attached to the beginning of all reels of film. Contains a start mark and numbers at each footage down to 3 ft from the start of the first frame of picture. Similar leaders are also attached to all soundtracks. In the US the term **projection leaders** is used. These are identified there as **Academy** or **SMPTE leaders** and further identified as **Head** or **Tail leaders.**

Level cut, straight cut or editorial cut (US terms)   A cut where sound and picture are cut at the same point.

Level synchronization   Where picture and soundtrack are kept in alignment. US term, **Editorial Sync.**

Library shot   Shot used in a film, but not taken specially for it; shot taken from a film or library source outside the actual unit producing a film.

Loop   Short length of film joined at its ends to form an endless loop so that it can be projected repetitively, either to enable actors to fit words to lip movements or to enable sound effects to be fitted. In the case of soundtracks, a loop is frequently made up of continuous sounds such as crowd noises, wind, sea breakers, etc. A loop plays continuously and can be mixed in with the others at any time during a sound mixing session.

M and E track   A mixed music and effects track which is free of voice-over narration. Essential if foreign-language versions are required.

Magnetic   Magnetic film stock, usually perforated, for sound recording.

Mag. stripe   Magnetic coating on the side of film used for sound recording.

Married print   A print where sound and picture are combined on the same piece of film stock. U.S. terms, **composite print** or **combined print**.

Master   A camera master is the original camera material, also known by the term **original**, particularly in the U.S.A. Master magnetic recording is the original sound recording.

Medium shot (Abbr. MS)   Shot taken with the camera not so far away from the subject as for a long-shot but not so close as for a close-up.

Mix   Another name for a **dissolve** (q.v.).

Mute   A picture negative or positive print without a soundtrack.

Negative   A piece of film where the tone values of the image are reversed. Black is white and white is black.

Negative cutter   The person who matches master and cutting copy.

Negative cutting   The matching of original negative (or colour master) to the edited cutting copy.

Optical (Effect)   Dissolves, fade-ins and outs, wipes and other special effects are known as opticals.

Optical dupe   Duplicate materials made in producing optical effects.

Optical soundtrack   A photographic soundtrack, printed. Sound modulations are visible.

Positive   Print.

Post-synchronization   Recording sound to a picture after the picture has been shot.

Release print   Projection print of a finished film.

Reversal film   A type of film stock which after exposure and processing produces a positive image instead of a negative.

Rushes   Film that has just been exposed by a film camera. In the case of a print, a print of scenes exactly as they were shot in the camera without any cutting or editing having taken place. Also known as **Dailies.**

Show print or release print   Projection print of a finished film.

Slate   See **Clapper board.**

Sound stripe   See **Magnetic stripe.**

Spacer or spacing   See **Leader.**

Stock shot   See **Library shot.**

Straight cut   See **Level cut.**

Trims   Unwanted portions of shots.

Wax pencil   A grease or wax pencil used for marking the edited **work print.** A yellow or white pencil may be used to indicate visual effects (such as fades, dissolves, etc.) and provide picture cues for any recording or mixing effects.

Work print   Print used for editing purposes. It is usually an ungraded print taken from all or part of the camera original. Also **Cutting copy.**

Appendix

Film running times and footages for 16 mm film
(Calculated to the nearest 1 ft)

Running time (mins)	Footage at 24 fps	Footage at 25 fps
1	36	37
2	72	75
3	108	112
4	144	150
5	180	187
6	216	225
7	252	262
8	288	300
9	324	337
10	360	375
15	540	563
20	720	750
25	900	938
30	1080	1126
35	1260	1313
40	1440	1500
45	1620	1687
50	1800	1876
55	1980	2063
60	2160	2250

Footage	Running time (min/sec) at 24 fps	Running time (min/sec) at 25 fps
1.16	0.2	0.1
2.16	0.3	0.3
3.16	0.5	0.4
4.16	0.6	0.6
5.16	0.8	0.8
6.16	0.10	0.9
7.16	0.12	0.11
8.16	0.13	0.12
9.16	0.15	0.14
10.16	0.17	0.16
25.16	0.42	0.40
50.16	1.23	1.20
75.16	2.5	2.0
100	2.47	2.40
150	4.10	4.0
200	5.33	5.20
250	6.57	6.40
300	8.20	8.0
350	9.43	9.20
400	11.7	10.40
450	12.30	12.0
500	13.53	13.20
550	15.16	14.40
600	16.39	16.0
650	18.2	17.20
700	19.25	18.40
750	20.48	20.0
800	22.11	21.20
850	23.34	22.40
900	24.57	24.0
950	26.20	25.20
1000	27.43	26.40
1500	41.36	40.0
1700	47.8	45.20
2000	55.26	53.20

Index